EINSTEIN'S RIDDLE

Conceived and produced by
Elwin Street Limited
144 Liverpool Road
London N1 1LA
www.elwinstreet.com

Published by Bloomsbury USA, New York

All papers used by Bloomsbury USA are natural, recyclable products
made from wood grown in well-managed forests. The
manufacturing processes conform to the environmental regulations
of the country of origin.

Library of Congress Control Number: 2008940802

ISBN-10 1-59691-665-6
ISBN-13 978-1-59691-665-4

First U.S. Edition 2009

Designed by Diana Sullada

10 9 8 7 6 5 4 3 2

Printed in China

EINSTEIN'S RIDDLE

RIDDLES, PARADOXES, AND CONUNDRUMS

TO *stretch* YOUR MIND

JEREMY STANGROOM

BLOOMSBURY

Contents

1
LOGIC AND PROBABILITY 8
Puzzles and riddles that can be solved
—if you reason like Einstein!

2
WHEN REASONING GOES WRONG 22
Puzzles and conundrums
that we should get right, but tend to get wrong

3
THE REAL WORLD 34
Puzzles and conundrums that
have practical implications

THINK RIDDLES ARE EASY?

It is rather shocking just how easy it is to get even a simple riddle wrong. Take this classic example:

> *A man points at a portrait, and then says:*
> *"Brothers and sisters have I none,*
> *but that man's father is my father's son".*
> *At whose picture is the man looking?*

There is a good chance that you think that he is looking at a picture of himself. If so, the good news is that you've hit upon what is probably the most common answer. The bad news is that you're wrong. In fact, the man is looking at a picture of his son. (If you're not convinced, substitute "me" for "my father's son," and read it through again.)

For those of us regularly bamboozled by this kind of thing, it is perhaps a comforting thought that riddles, paradoxes, and conundrums have been confounding people since the time of the Ancient Greeks. Zeno of Elea mused that Achilles could never catch a tortoise in a race, since whenever he reached a point where the tortoise had been, the tortoise would have moved on, even if by only a fraction. Zeno's Paradox, as it is called, is still troubling people more than 2,000 years after it was originally posed. It belongs to a class of puzzles that are more than simple brain-teasers.

The problems that these paradoxes pose go right to the heart of questions to do with logic, time, motion, and language. So there's a challenge here: if you're able to figure out an elegant solution to them, you will have done better than many of the great minds who have pondered them over the past two millennia.

As you work through this book, you'll find some of the puzzles easy, some difficult, and others maddeningly difficult. At times, you'll be infuriated, perhaps convinced that the "correct" answer to a riddle is nothing of the sort. At other times, you'll be puzzled in a deep way—some paradoxes are just paradoxical all the way down. But my hope is that you will be continuously stimulated and challenged by the riddles, paradoxes, and conundrums that have diverted and engaged some of history's greatest minds.

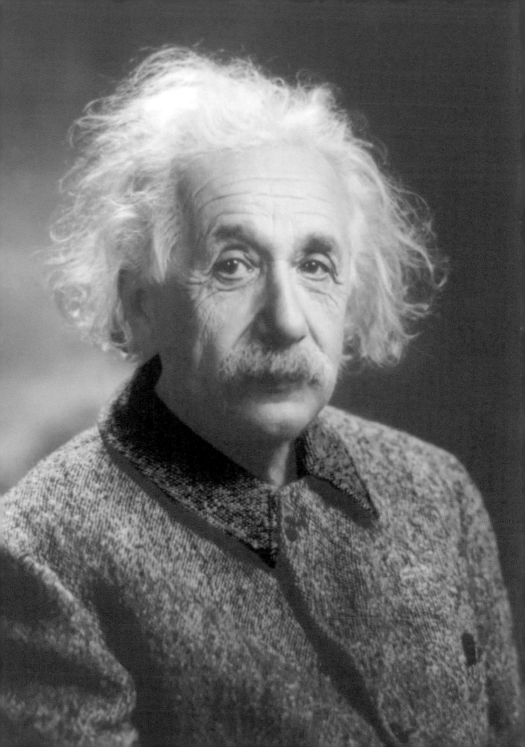

1

LOGIC AND PROBABILITY

LOGIC, n.

*The art of thinking and reasoning in strict accordance with
the limitations and incapacities of human misunderstanding.*

AMBROSE BIERCE: *THE DEVIL'S DICTIONARY*

We're going to start things off nice and easy. There is nothing
underhanded or tricksy about the puzzles and conundrums
that appear in this section. They are straightforward tests of
logic and probability. Happily, they all have solutions—which
is not true of some of the conundrums that appear later in the
book—which means that if you think about them carefully, you
should be able to work out the right answers.

However, we're talking "nice and easy" in a relative sense
here. Most people just aren't that smart when it comes to logic,
so many tend to get these kinds of puzzles wrong. The Monty
Hall problem, for example, seemingly an easy test of our
ability to calculate probabilities, has bamboozled some of the
best mathematical minds in the business. And Einstein's
Riddle is reckoned to be one of the hardest straight logic tests
ever devised.

So if you manage to get the correct solution to more than
one or two of these, you're doing well. But rest assured, the
puzzles and conundrums in this section are just the beginning.

EINSTEIN'S RIDDLE

Are you smart enough to solve the world's hardest riddle? According to legend, this riddle was devised by Albert Einstein as a child. It is said that only about 2 percent of the population would be able to work out the correct answer. There are no tricks here. There is only one answer. It just requires the cool application of logic to solve. And a lot of patience.

There are five houses painted five different colors. A person with a different nationality lives in each house. The five house owners each drink a certain type of beverage, play a certain sport, and keep a certain pet. No owners have the same pet, play the same sport, or drink the same beverage.

Who owns the fish?

THE FACTS

1. The Briton lives in the red house.
2. The Swede keeps dogs as pets.
3. The Dane drinks tea.
4. The green house is on the left of the white house.
5. The owner of the green house drinks coffee.
6. The person who plays football rears birds.
7. The owner of the yellow house plays baseball.
8. The man living in the center house drinks milk.
9. The Norwegian lives in the first house.
10. The man who plays volleyball lives next to the one who keeps cats.
11. The man who keeps the horse lives next to the man who plays baseball.
12. The owner who plays tennis drinks beer.
13. The German plays hockey.
14. The Norwegian lives next to the blue house.
15. The man who plays volleyball has a neighbor who drinks water.

The key to solving this riddle is to create a grid. One column for each of the five houses, and five rows for nationality, house color, type of beverage, type of sport, and kind of pet.

TIPS TO GET YOU STARTED

Fact # 8 states that the man in the center house drinks milk, and Fact # 9 states that the person living in the first house is Norwegian, so we can add these to the grid:

	HOUSE 1	HOUSE 2	HOUSE 3	HOUSE 4	HOUSE 5
NATIONALITY	*Norweigan*				
COLOR					
BEVERAGE			*milk*		
SPORT					
PET					

From here it is just a matter of applying logic to fill out the grid on the basis of the clues. Good luck!

(SOLUTION ON PAGE 84)

QUICKIE 1

You have two containers, one of which
will hold three gallons of water,
the other five gallons of water. You need exactly
four gallons of water.

*How do you use these two containers
to measure out the four gallons?*

(SOLUTIONS ON PAGE 136)

QUICKIE 2

Trains travel from London to Southampton
all through the day, always on the same track,
always going nonstop, and at the same speed.
The two P.M. train took eighty minutes
to complete the trip, but the four P.M. train
took an hour and twenty minutes.

Why?

FERRARI OR GOAT?
THE MONTY HALL PROBLEM

William Capra was overjoyed when he was selected to appear on "Ferrari or Goat?," television's number one quiz show, in which contestants either drive away in a shiny new car, or walk away, rather sheepishly, with a recalcitrant four-legged companion in tow. William defers to no man in his fondness for goats, but he'd still on balance prefer to win the Ferrari. Unhappily, this seems rather unlikely right now, since he is flummoxed by a conundrum that has been set by the game show host Monty Hall.

There are three doors. Behind one door is the car, behind the other two, goats. There is no pattern to this, the car and the goats have been randomly allocated. William must choose a door. Monty Hall, who knows what is behind the doors, will then open one of the two remaining doors and he has to reveal a goat. William then must decide whether to stick with his original choice, or to switch to the remaining door.

Monty Hall advises William that most people get this puzzle wrong. William is told that when the puzzle was featured in a column by Marilyn vos Savant in *Parade* magazine, some 10,000 readers, including hundreds of mathematicians, wrote in to complain, incorrectly, and often none too politely, that the solution that she had offered was wrong.

So how should William answer to avoid becoming just another person beaten by the conundrum? If he wants to maximize his chances of winning the Ferrari, should he stick with his original choice, or switch to the remaining door? And what is the reason for the choice he should make?

(SOLUTION ON PAGE 86)

Door #1   Door #2   Door #3

BERTRAND'S BOX

The great adventurer Iowa Jones is facing a dilemma. He has spent a lifetime searching for the Twin Pearls of Des Moines, and has finally tracked them down. But there's a problem. He knows that they are in one of three caskets, each of which has two drawers, but he doesn't know which casket. What's more, when he prizes open one of the drawers, he finds what looks like one of the Twin Pearls, together with a note that sends chills running down his spine.

Dear Great Adventurer,
Before you there are three caskets. One casket contains the Twin Pearls of Des Moines, a single pearl in each drawer. Another casket contains a pearl in one drawer, and a piece of coal in the other. The final casket contains two pieces of coal, one in each drawer. Unfortunately, there is no way of telling the three pearls apart: you only know that you've got the genuine Des Moines pearls by the fact that they are in the same casket. And there's one final thing: you are only able to open one more drawer—get it wrong, and all three caskets will self-destruct.

Iowa Jones circles the caskets considering his options, and then brings his hammer down hard on the lock of the second drawer of the casket he has already opened.

What is the probability that Iowa Jones will find a second pearl in the casket, and thereby claim his long sought-after prize?

(SOLUTION ON PAGE 90)

BOY OR GIRL PUZZLE

Martin Moneta has a perplexing problem. He's spent six months trekking in the Andes, and during this time he seems to have forgotten the sex of his children. He knows he has two children, and that one of them is a boy. But he isn't sure whether the other child is a boy or a girl.

The good news is that he has managed to keep this rather embarrassing memory lapse a secret. The bad news is that he's now at the airport awaiting a flight home, which means that he really ought to buy his children a gift or two. This presents a problem: a boy isn't going to take too kindly to receiving a Barbie Doll, and a girl isn't much going to like getting a model of the Six Million Dollar Man (Martin's other problem is that he still thinks it's the 1970s.)

Martin decides that probability theory is his best chance here. He needs to determine whether it is more likely that his child of currently indeterminate sex is a boy or a girl. Then he can take a chance on the right kind of present.

He ponders for a little while, and decides that since at least one of his two children is a boy, it is more likely that the other child is a girl than a boy.

Is he right? And if so, why?

(SOLUTION ON PAGE 92)

CHAPTER 1

QUICKIE 3

The old king decides to set a task to determine
which of his two sons will inherit his kingdom.
He tells them that the son whose horse is last to reach
the church on the hill will become the next king.
His younger son immediately jumps on a horse
and gallops toward the church at top speed.
The king is good to his word,
and leaves him his kingdom.

Why?

(SOLUTIONS ON PAGE 136)

QUICKIE 4

Rachel drives 113 miles from Pittsburgh to Cleveland
averaging thirty miles per hour.

*How fast must she drive on the return trip
to average sixty miles per hour overall?*

HOW OLD ARE THEY?

Alex Gibbon, sociologist and radical thinker, has run into a spot of bother with his latest research project on the development of revolutionary consciousness in rural Devon. He has spent a happy morning going from door to door talking to people about the imminent collapse of capitalism—something that sociologists the world over have been looking forward to since 1867—but is having a little trouble with his final conversation of the day.

The conversation had started off normally enough. Gibbon had knocked on the door, and then after introducing himself, had asked the person who answered how many people were living in the house. He was told that there were three people living there. In order to test his theory that revolutionary politics attracts all age groups, and not just dreamy teenagers, Gibbon enquired about their ages. It was then that things became a little odd. He was informed that the product of their ages (i.e., their ages multiplied together) is 225; and the sum of their ages (i.e., their ages added together) is the same as the house number.

Gibbon is flummoxed. He peers at the house number, and notes it down, but can't begin to work out how he's supposed to determine anybody's age from the information he's been given. He is just about to give up when a voice booms from down the garden path: "Ask her whether she's much older than her siblings!" Gibbon spins around to find a policeman looking at him insistently. Fearing institutional oppression, he does as he is told, and asks the question. The response comes back: "Yes."

Gibbon can't see how knowing this helps him, but the policeman, a certain Inspector Horse, explains how he can now work out how old the people are who live in the house.

What does Horse explain to him?
How old are the people in the house?

(SOLUTION ON PAGE 94)

2

WHEN REASONING GOES WRONG

*It has been said that man is a rational animal. All my life I have been
searching for evidence which could support this.*
BERTRAND RUSSELL: *UNPOPULAR ESSAYS*

Bertrand Russell had plenty of reason to be pessimistic about the
capacity of human beings to be rational. We just very easily fall
into error and confusion. Check out this argument, for example:

Every person is a ray of sunshine.

Every person is a being of light and shade.

Therefore every being of light and shade is a ray of sunshine.

Do you think it is valid? Does the conclusion that every
being of light and shade is a ray of sunshine necessarily follow
from the premises?

If you think it is valid, then you've made a logical error.
Here's the same argument with different terms:

Every horse is a mammal.

Every horse is a four-legged creature.

Therefore every four-legged creature is a mammal.

If you think that this is the case, then you probably don't
want to try teaching zoology to a tortoise!

Of course, it's possible that you got this right, and that
you're now feeling confident. If so, then let's hope that your
confidence is not misplaced, since the vast majority of people
get the puzzles and conundrums in this section wrong.

ELEMENTARY, MY DEAR WASON

Police Officer Jack Dawe has had enough of traffic duty and rescuing runaway parrots, so he is delighted when he spots a notice in *Police Gazette* advertizing a detective position with the Greater Chudleigh constabulary. He applies for the job, and is offered an interview, but is told that he must first pass an aptitude test to determine whether he has the logic skills necessary to be a top-notch detective.

Officer Dawe has always rather considered himself a clever fellow, so he's confident that he'll easily pass the test, and go on to become a detective. His confidence remains high when it becomes clear what is involved.

He is presented with four playing cards, and told that they have been manufactured according to a very strict rule:

> If a card has a circle on one side, then it has the color yellow on the other.

He is informed that it has already been established that every card has a shape on one side and a color on the other. To pass the test, Jack Dawe simply has to identify which of the four cards it is necessary to turn over—and only that or those cards—in order to determine whether the manufacturing rule has been upheld.

The four cards are as follows:

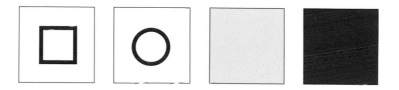

Officer Dawe can hardly believe his luck. A brilliant mind such as his will surely have no difficulty with this simple test. However, as he is about to answer, the test invigilator mentions that typically only 20 percent of applicants tend to get this test right. Apparently, we're not very good at this kind of logic.

Officer Dawe hesitates, and then makes his choice . . .

Which card or cards does he need to have turned over in order to check whether the manufacturing rule has been upheld, and thereby pass his aptitude test?

(SOLUTION ON PAGE 96)

WHAT DOES MARY DO?

Mary Davies is 32 years old, not married, very outspoken, and highly intelligent. She has a degree in sociology. Mary was actively involved in student politics at university, and she is particularly concerned with issues to do with racism and poverty. She also took part in animal rights, pro-choice, anti-globalization, and anti-nuclear demonstrations. She is now concentrating on environmental issues such as renewable energy and climate change.

There are four statements about Mary below. On the basis of the information provided above, it is your job to judge how likely each statement is to be true, using this scale:

> 1 – Very Probable; 2 – Probable; 3 – Possible;
> 4 – Unlikely; 5 – Very Unlikely

Statement	How likely to be true?
1. Mary is a psychiatric social worker	
2. Mary is a bank clerk	
3. Mary is an insurance salesperson	
4. Mary is a bank clerk and active in the feminist movement	

Which statement about Mary is most likely to be true?

Perhaps you're thinking that there is no right or wrong answer here. It just seems obvious that we can't know for certain what Mary is doing with her life on the basis of such a short description. This is true, of course, but it is also true that most people go wrong when thinking about what Mary is likely to be doing now.

So, in addition to judging how likely each statement is to be true, see if you can work out how people tend to go wrong when thinking about what Mary might be doing.

(SOLUTION ON PAGE 98)

THE GAMBLER'S MISTAKE

Karen Jones is a keen soccer fan. She watches British games on television, and supports Manchester United. One morning, she receives an e-mail that says simply:

> October 12th—Derby County to win.

She thinks little more about it, but she takes note that Derby do indeed win on that date, a result which many people beforehand would have considered more than a little unlikely.

The next week she receives a similar e-mail predicting a victory for Middlesbrough and, sure enough, they win their game, too. The third week, Karen receives another prediction, and again it turns out to be correct, as does the prediction that arrives in the fourth week.

By now, Karen's curiosity is more than a little piqued. Not only has she seemingly attracted the attention of the world's only reliable psychic but if she places a few bets she could make some money out of these predictions. Karen's a cautious woman, and not entirely convinced that the outcome of any soccer match is preordained, so she holds off for the time being.

But the pattern continues. Each week an e-mail arrives predicting the result of a game. And each week the prediction is correct. Then on the 10th week the e-mail changes. This time it says:

> To receive your final prediction you must pay $250
> via PayMate to Soccer Predictions Ltd.

Karen curses the fact that she has not previously placed a bet but then she thinks, well, $250 is not so much money, and a $2,000 bet would mean quite a nice return. She calculates that the odds of correctly predicting the outcome of nine games in a row are about 1 in 7,000 (assuming the results are random), which surely means that Soccer Predictions Ltd must have some inside knowledge. So she pays the fee, receives her prediction, and places her bet.

But then she thinks some more about what has happened, and her mind drifts to the classes on probability she took in college, which is when she realizes that she has been very daft and fallen into a probability trap. Soccer Predictions Ltd have no idea who is going to win the next game. She has been conned.

What has Karen has worked out?

(SOLUTION ON PAGE 99)

THE THIEVING CLOWN

The trainee clowns at Bozo College are in a state of shock. A thief has deprived the college of 873 yellow balloons and a broken-down balloon pump. Happily, there was a witness to the crime, who has stated that the thief was wearing the College's clown uniform and had a red nose. Previous research has shown that on 80 percent of occasions witnesses will correctly identify the color of the nose of a clown involved in committing a crime. It is also known that 85 percent of the clowns at Bozo College have blue noses and that 15 percent have red noses.

What is the probability that the thief had a red nose (assuming that the witness is telling the truth about what he thinks he saw)?

TIPS TO GET YOU STARTED
The key to answering this question is to realize that it is not possible to rely upon the accuracy of the witness statement alone (so if you think that the probability is most likely 80 percent then you're wrong). Rather, it is necessary to take into account the overall distribution of clowns with blue and red noses at Bozo College.

(SOLUTION ON PAGE 100)

Quickie 5

A zookeeper has lost the ability
to distinguish between elephants and emus.
However, he is able to count eyes and feet.
He counts fifty-eight eyes and eighty-four feet.

*How many elephants
and how many emus
are there?*

(SOLUTIONS ON PAGE 137)

Quickie 6

Some bacteria in a bowl divide themselves
every minute in two equal parts that are the
same size as the original bacteria, and which
also divide the next minute and so on.
The bowl in which this is occurring
is full at twelve P.M.

When was it half full?

THE DISAPPEARING DOLLAR

Three traveling salesmen check into a hotel. Not wanting to max out their expense accounts, they decide to share one room. They pay $30 to the manager and head off to raid the mini-bar. The manager then realizes that the weekday rate for the room is only $25, so he gives $5 to the bellboy to return to the men. The bellboy tries to work out how to split $5 three ways, but fails, so he pockets $2, and gives $1 each to the salesmen.

But there's a problem here. It seems that a dollar has gone missing. The three salesmen started off by paying the hotel $30 ($10 each). The manager of the hotel then gave $5 of $30 to the bellboy, who took $2 for himself and gave the remaining $3 back to the men ($1 to each man). Each salesman originally paid $10 (3 x $10 = $30), and has received $1 back, which means that each man has now paid $9 to the hotel.

So we've got the $27 that the salesmen have paid (3 x $9) and the $2 dollars the bell boy has pocketed. This accounts for $29. But the salesmen originally gave the hotel $30.

Where's the missing dollar gone?

(SOLUTION ON PAGE 102)

Quickie 7

There are two swans
in front of a swan,
two swans behind a swan,
and one swan in the middle.

How many swans are there?

(SOLUTIONS ON PAGE 137)

?

Quickie 8

Two boys are born
to the same mother,
on the same day,
at the same time,
in the same year
and yet they're not twins.

How can this be?

?

THE REAL WORLD

Logic is one thing and commonsense another.

ELBERT HUBBARD· *THE NOTE BOOK*

It is possible that you think that the puzzles and conundrums featured in this book have little relevance to the business of everyday life. They may be diverting, and they may provide a useful mental workout, but the challenges they pose are not the kind of thing you come across as you go about your daily business. The temptation is to suppose, as Elbert Hubbard put it, that logic is one thing, commonsense quite another.

However, you should not be too quick to draw this conclusion. Although it is true that you're probably never going to have to figure out who owns a fish on the basis of a story about houses and their occupants, it is also the case that the ability to calculate probabilities, to work through various decision-making scenarios, and to spot faulty reasoning has real-world implications. Certainly, if you gamble or ever form part of a jury in a court case, then you'll do well to cultivate these abilities.

So if you don't cope so well with the real-world problems featured in this section, perhaps you should exercise caution before comforting yourself with the thought that logic and rationality are non-essential luxuries. It might be true that logic is one thing and commonsense another, but to choose commonsense over logic might not be entirely sensible.

THE PRISONER'S DILEMMA

Arthur Achilles and Hector House have been arrested by the police for brawling outside the Troy Arms. It turns out that they came to blows after their planned robbery of a marina went wrong when the sea turned mysteriously wine-dark. The police, though, do not have enough evidence to prosecute Arthur and Hector for the marina robbery, so they come up with a cunning plan. They separate the two prisoners, and independently offer them the following deal.

If one testifies that the other was involved in the marina robbery, and the other remains silent, the betrayer will be set free, while his silent accomplice will spend the next ten years in prison. If both remain silent, then both of them will only spend six months in jail for their fighting. However, if they both betray the other, then each will receive a five-year prison sentence. Hector and Arthur must choose whether to betray each other or to remain silent.

They have no way of communicating, and no way of knowing what the other will do. This presents them both with a dilemma.

Should they keep quiet and hope that their partner in crime does the same? Or should they talk faster than a rabbit explaining the benefits of a vegetarian diet to a fox?

TIPS TO GET YOU STARTED

The various possibilities look like this:

	HECTOR REMAINS SILENT	HECTOR SINGS LIKE A BIRD
ARTHUR REMAINS SILENT	*Both get 6 months in jail.*	*Arthur gets 10 years in jail. Hector goes free.*
ARTHUR SINGS LIKE A BIRD	*Arthur goes free. Hector gets 10 years in jail.*	*Both get 5 years in jail.*

(SOLUTION ON PAGE 104)

THE DOLLAR AUCTION

Ronald Plump has come up with a perfect plan to make money. He's going to sell dollar notes at auction. Admittedly, at first glance, this does not seem like a perfect plan. But Plump has developed some special rules for his auction: The dollar will be won by the highest bidder, but the next highest bidder must also pay the amount that they bid and, crucially, they will get nothing in return.

If it is not clear how this will make money, then consider how the auction is likely to unfold. Let's assume that the first bid is for 1 cent, with the bidder hoping to make 99 cents as profit. No doubt, other players will very quickly make higher bids, reckoning that smaller profits are still worthwhile. Very soon, a series of bids will become established.

However, this results in a problem when the bidding hits 99 cents. The player who made the preceding bid—perhaps 98 cents—stands to lose their money unless they make a one-dollar bid. Clearly, from their point of view it is better to break even than to lose 98 cents by not bidding. However, this then places the player who had previously bid 99 cents in exactly the same situation. They're better off bidding $1.01, which means a one-cent loss, than not bidding, and thereby losing 99 cents. The point is that this pattern might continue indefinitely with only the auctioneer standing to gain.

Has Ronald Plump hit upon the perfect plan to make money? Or is there a way that the bidders can escape the trap that he has set?

(SOLUTION ON PAGE 106)

CHAPTER 3

QUICKIE 9

You are in front of two doors;
behind one door is a ferocious lion,
behind the other door, a pot of gold.
The doors are watched over by two guards.
You are allowed to ask just one question.
One guard always tells the truth.
The other guard always lies.

*What should you ask in order to
determine which door
the pot of gold lies behind?*

(SOLUTIONS ON PAGE 138)

QUICKIE 10

You have eight books.

*How many ways
can you arrange them
left to right on a shelf?*

THE GAMBLER'S FALLACY

Bobby de Faro has come up with the perfect plan to scam the new Super Casino. It is brilliant in its simplicity. In fact, all it requires is a roulette table, a little money, and a lot of nous.

The plan has two elements. First, de Faro will skulk around the casino's roulette tables until he observes a run of wins on either red or black. He will then begin to bet on the other color, reasoning as follows. The probability that the ball will fall on either a black number or a red number is approximately 50-50 for each number (it's not exactly 50-50, because there's a house number, zero or double zero). This means, on average, that if the wheel is spun twenty times it is to be expected that the ball will settle on red ten times and on black ten times. Therefore, if there has been a run on either black or red, it is sensible to bet on the other color, since things are bound to even out over time. De Faro believes that he will win enough this way to put the second element of his plan into operation.

The second element involves betting on black, and then doubling the bet if he loses, so that when he eventually wins, he will recoup all his previous losses, plus make a profit equivalent to the original stake.

It is de Faro's belief that the laws of probability mean that his plan cannot fail.

Profit and losses for a series of winning bets
(assuming that the odds are even).

	STAKE (Doubled from previous bets)	WINNINGS	LOSSES (from previous bets placed)	TOTAL PROFIT
1ST BET WINS	2	2	—	2
2ND BET WINS	4	4	2	2
3RD BET WINS	8	8	6	2
4TH BET WINS	16	16	14	2
5TH BET WINS	32	32	30	2
6TH BET WINS	64	64	62	2

A winning run on black or red is not going to last forever, so it makes sense to bet on the other color. And in a game where there is a 50-50 chance of winning, a losing run will soon end, so if you double your bet each time you lose, you will quickly win your money back, plus make a profit.

Has de Faro come up with the perfect scam? Or is his knowledge of probability as empty as a squirrel with a nut allergy?

(SOLUTION ON PAGE 107)

LIES, DAMNED LIES, AND STATISTICS

Jim and Jules are fierce rivals in the village of Chudleigh-by-the-Pond. They compete endlessly with each other to see who can ring the village bell most vigorously; they aim to outdo each other each year in the annual pin-the-tail-on-the-donkey contest; and they inevitably chase the same village girls. However, most of all they strive to win the Catherine Moreau trophy, which is awarded to the member of the village quiz team who has the highest average score in a series of games against rival villages Chudleigh-by-the-Lake and Chudleigh-by-the-Ocean.

This year's contest has been particularly keenly fought, and the boys are on edge when Chudleigh-by-the-Pond's mayor gets up to announce the result to a packed meeting at the Village Hall.

The results show that Jim has a better average than Jules against both the rival villages, so Jim is declared the winner, and presented with the trophy. However, his rather exuberant victory jig is interrupted by a voice booming from the back of the hall. Inspector Horse, the village policeman, and amateur philosopher, demands to speak to the mayor. After a lengthy conversation with Horse, and much scratching of the mayoral hair, the Mayor sensationally reverses her decision, declaring that the results in fact show that Jules is the winner.

Opponent: Chudleigh-by-the-Lake

	JIM	JULES
GAMES PLAYED	10	6
TOTAL SCORE	500	270
AVERAGE	50	45

Opponent: Chudleigh-by-the-Ocean

	JIM	JULES
GAMES PLAYED	4	10
TOTAL SCORE	320	700
AVERAGE	80	70

This news is greeted with dismay by Jim, and even Jules manages only a tentative victory jig, unable quite to believe that he is actually the winner.

What did Inspector Horse reveal about the results that has led the Mayor to change her mind and declare Jules the winner?

(SOLUTION ON PAGE 108)

THE PARADOX OF DETERRENCE

Stanley Love is very proud of the pumpkins he has been growing for the Meddybemps Annual Weigh-Off. Consequently, he is devastated one morning to discover that one of his pumpkins has been tagged by the Meddy Posse, a local gang. Love is aware that pumpkin tagging is a growing problem in the town, so he decides to implement a deterrent against future raids. To this end, he erects large signs around his property, which state that his pumpkins have been wired up to an electrical generator, and that he will turn on the current if he sees anybody interfering with them.

The Meddy Posse, though, are not the types to be deterred by a few thousand volts of electricity, so the next night they're back inside Love's pumpkin sanctuary, busily leaving their mark on his prized Atlantic Giants. Stanley Love is watching all this from behind the generator, and he is about to make good on his promise to switch on the current, when he realizes something: he doesn't want to. The deterrent has failed, the gang have already defaced his pumpkins, so there seems to be little point in inflicting suffering upon them.

Stanley then begins to think about the nature of deterrence in general. It seems to him that there is a paradox lurking around the idea that it is possible to deter. If it is only possible to deter by threatening a sanction you know you won't want to carry out, then you can't form the intention to apply the sanction in the first place (because you know that you're not going to want to carry it out). But a deterrent depends upon all parties being aware that there is a true intention to respond in some specific way.

Is this a genuine paradox? Does it undermine the whole idea of a successful deterrent? Or is there a way we can still employ deterrents?

(SOLUTION ON PAGE 110)

THE PARADOX OF JURISDICTION

Judge Judy Solomon, Greater Bovey's finest legal brain, has been asked for her advice on a perplexing problem. A number of years previously, Lesser Bovey's ceremonial parrot, Icarus, had been horribly wounded during an autumn pheasant shoot in Chudleigh-by-the-Pond. He was rushed back to Lesser Bovey, where he received the best medical care available, but sadly he succumbed to his wounds the next spring. At the time, it was not clear who was responsible for shooting down Icarus. However, Detective Jack Dawe, keen to impress after securing a position with the Greater Chudleigh constabulary, has recently discovered that the culprit was local landowner, Billy Blacklaw, who, somewhat ironically, died of yellow fever just a few weeks after the shooting.

At first, Detective Dawe was chuffed that he had solved the case. However, the more he has thought about it, the less sure he is that he knows quite who killed Icarus, or indeed, where or when he was killed. The problem is as follows:

Icarus can't have been killed in the autumn, at the time of the original shooting, because he was still alive in the autumn. However, he can't have been killed in the spring either, because Billy Blacklaw was dead by then, and a dead person can't kill. But if he wasn't killed in the autumn or the spring, when was he killed?

Moreover, if Icarus wasn't killed in the autumn, then he can't have been killed in Chudleigh-by-the Pond, since that is the only time he had been to Chudleigh. But equally, he can't have been killed in Lesser Bovey, because Billy Blacklaw, who inflicted his wounds, never visited the village, and anyway, he was dead by the time Icarus died.

So Detective Jack Dawe has three very simple questions for Judge Solomon.

Who killed Icarus? When was he killed?
And where was he killed?

(SOLUTION ON PAGE 112)

Alfred de Musset.

MOTION, INFINITY, AND VAGUENESS

I cannot help it—in spite of myself, infinity torments me.

ALFRED DE MUSSET: *L'ESPOIR EN DIEU*

At first sight, it might seem a little esoteric to include a selection of puzzles and conundrums on the subject of motion, infinity, and vagueness. In fact, however, there is a good chance that you've already come across some of the challenges posed by these concepts.

Take the idea of infinity, for example. Imagine the following scenario: time is infinite. It reaches back indefinitely into the past and extends indefinitely into the future. The amount of matter in the universe though is only finite: there is a fixed amount, and it cannot be altered. The consequence of these two facts is—or seems to be—that every possible arrangement of matter will occur at some point in time, and not only once, but on an infinite number of occasions. Moreover, because time reaches back infinitely into the past, it follows that every possible arrangement of matter has already occurred an infinite number of times. This means, of course, that this is not the first time you've read this book.

If this kind of thought experiment is familiar to you, then you already have a sense of the kinds of puzzles featured in this section. Happily, though, likely this is not because you have already read this book an infinite number of times . . .

BALD MAN LOGIC

Samson prides himself on his full head of hair. He is rather perturbed then when he catches his girlfriend Delilah peering at his head, muttering something about baldness. Samson has studied philosophy at Canaan University, so he is confident that he can prove that no matter how much hair he loses, he will never be bald.

SAMSON: *Is a man with 10,000 hairs on his head bald?*

DELILAH: *Such a man is clearly blessed with a full head of hair.*

SAMSON: *Could taking one hair from such a head ever make the difference between a man being not-bald and bald?*

DELILAH: *One hair is nothing to such a man.*

SAMSON: *So a man with 9,999 hairs is not bald?*

DELILAH: *He is not.*

SAMSON: *9,998 hairs?*

DELILAH: *Not bald.*

SAMSON: *9,997 hairs?*

DELILAH: *Hang on a minute, Samson, you're going to count all the way down to zero hairs, and claim that a man with no hair is not bald. But that's ridiculous!*

SAMSON: *It is not ridiculous at all, Delilah. You have insisted that taking one hair from a man who is not bald could never make enough difference to render him bald. My reasoning is impeccable. I will never be bald.*

DELILAH: <Wanders off looking for a large pair of scissors.>

Where has Samson got his logic wrong?
Surely it cannot be true that he will never be bald.
Can it?

(SOLUTION ON PAGE 114)

DOLLY'S CAT AND THE SHIP OF THESEUS

Dolly Aires is hopelessly in love with her cat, Montmorency. Consequently, she is acutely aware that he is likely to shuffle off his mortal coil before she meets her own demise. So she comes up with a plan to ensure a longer future together. Her plan is to clone Montmorency's body parts and replace them as they wear out. She's a little worried that he might be changed in some way by it, so she decides that an experimental approach is the best way to proceed.

She starts by replacing his tail. His new tail is perhaps a little more lustrous than his old tail, but he appears still to be Montmorency. Next she replaces his legs. No problem, he hardly seems to notice the difference. When he doesn't seem to show any character changes even after replacing his head, she presses on with her plan, until she has replaced every bit of Montmorency's body with new parts.

Dolly is very happy that she'll be able to extend Montmorency's life significantly this way. However, her happiness turns to horror a few weeks later after she attends a public lecture on Greek philosophy. It seems at least possible that Montmorency is not Montmorency at all, but rather a furry imposter with the same taste in gourmet sardines.

What has Dolly figured out that has disturbed her so greatly? And is she right to worry?

(SOLUTION ON PAGE 116)

QUICKIE 11

There are a total of thirty-one games
in a knock-out tennis tournament
(i.e., once a player loses then they are
out of the tournament).

How many players take part in the tournament?

(SOLUTIONS ON PAGE 139)

QUICKIE 12

A man lives on the thirteenth floor of a downtown apartment
block. Every weekday he takes the elevator to go down to the
ground floor to go to work. When he returns, he takes the
elevator to the eighth floor and then walks up the stairs to
reach his apartment on the thirteenth floor. If it is raining,
he does the same thing, except he takes the elevator to the
tenth floor before walking.

He hates walking, so why does he do it?

HOTEL INFINITY

Hotelier Basil Sinclair is the proud owner of a very unusual hotel. Hotel Infinity, as it is called, has an infinite number of rooms. Sinclair has always felt confident that his advertizing slogan—"We've always got room for you"—will hold true. However, today he is feeling just a little nervous. Inspector Horse, local amateur philosopher and polymath, has hired the hotel's conference room to give a grand lecture and, rather surprisingly, an infinite number of guests have arrived at the hotel in order to attend the talk. This means that all the rooms at Hotel Infinity are occupied.

Sinclair is peering nervously out of the hotel lobby window, when, to his horror, he spies a new problem: a cavalcade of coaches heading up the hotel driveway. His face drops as another infinitely large group of people disembark and head towards the hotel's revolving doors. Some considerable time later, they are all crowded around the hotel reception desk, demanding rooms, and angrily citing Sinclair's advertizing slogan when he tells them that the hotel is currently fully booked for the talk.

Luckily, Inspector Horse has been observing proceedings from the sidelines. He steps into the fray and announces that there is a way that the hotel can successfully accommodate an infinite number of new guests, and what's more, it can do so in such a way so as to ensure that nobody ends up with a stranger in their bed. Horse indicates that the key to solving the overcrowding problem is to recognize that at Hotel Infinity the fact that every room is occupied does not mean that there is no room for further guests.

How does Inspector Horse think that Hotel Infinity can accommodate an infinite number of new guests?

(SOLUTION ON PAGE 118)

ZENO AND THE THREE-LEGGED RACE

Normally the annual three-legged race at the Carnival of Phidippides goes off without a hitch. This year, however, an unfortunate dispute left competitors hopping mad and marred the event. The brouhaha started when a philosopher in the crowd objected to a five-legged competitor being given a head start. He claimed, rather implausibly, that it wasn't clear that the other competitors in the race would ever be able to catch their five-legged adversary. He explained that this issue had been explored by the Greeks in a series of experiments with tortoises.

Imagine that Achilles, swift-of-foot and light-of-finger, is taking on a tortoise in a race, and that he gives the tortoise a head start. Although Achilles is much faster than the tortoise, it is possible that he'll never be able to catch his dawdling opponent. This possibility rests on the fact that whenever Achilles reaches a point where the tortoise has been, the tortoise will have moved on a little further, even if only by a small amount.

The diagram below will make this clear.

t1

t2

t3

t4

At the beginning of the race (t1), the tortoise has a large lead. Very rapidly, Achilles gets to the point where the tortoise had started the race, but the tortoise has moved forward (t2). By t3, Achilles reaches where the tortoise was at t2, but again the reptilian blighter has gone a bit further. It seems that this pattern will continue indefinitely, with Achilles getting ever closer, but never actually catching the tortoise.

The philosopher explains all this to the competitors in the three-legged race. They are puzzled, but not convinced. However, when he challenges them to identify where his reasoning has gone wrong, they are unable to do so.

What should they have told him? How did the Greeks get it wrong? After all, it is surely the case that a tortoise is not going to win every race in which it is given a head start.

(SOLUTION ON PAGE 120)

5

PHILOSOPHICAL CONUNDRUMS

*One cannot conceive anything so strange and so implausible
that it has not already been said by one philosopher or another.*

RENE DESCARTES: *DISCOURSE ON METHOD*

For philosophers, puzzles and conundrums are not mere trifling distractions, but rather the potential source of insights that lead to developments in our knowledge of the world. Russell's Paradox, for example, provoked a revolution at the beginning of the twentieth century in the way that philosophers and mathematicians understood the nature of sets. Similarly, Zeno's Paradox, which appears in the previous chapter, but which is also properly philosophical, was partly responsible for developments in the nineteenth century in the way that mathematics treated the concept of infinity.

Not all the puzzles and conundrums in this section—or indeed, in the previous and succeeding sections—have definitive answers. So you should not be discouraged if you find yourself bamboozled and frustrated by problems that seem to be intractable. The Liar's Paradox, a classic philosophical conundrum, was first posed nearly 2,500 years ago, and yet to date there is no general agreement about how it should be solved. So if you get stuck, console yourself with the thought that many of the greatest minds in history have wrestled with these problems and come up short.

THE LIBRARIAN'S DILEMMA

Alexandra Pergamon has just been appointed Cataloguer-in-Chief at the world-renowned Lesser Bovey Library. The first task that she sets herself is to create a master catalogue of all the existing library catalogues. However, when she looks at the catalogues, which list the books in the library's various special collections, she notes that some of them list themselves as part of the collection that they detail, and some do not.

This offends her sense of order, so she decides that really she needs two master catalogues: the first for all the catalogues in the library that include a reference to themselves within their pages, and the second for the catalogues that do not.

Having made this decision, she sets to work. On finishing the first catalogue, she decides that since a master catalogue is a catalogue, it should include itself in its list of catalogues, so she adds a reference to itself. She then begins work on the second master catalogue. A few hours later, the job is done, except, as with the first master catalogue, she has to add a reference to itself within its list of catalogues. However, she quickly realizes that things aren't quite so simple with the second master catalogue. As far as she can determine, she can neither add the reference to itself, nor leave it out. In fact, she seems to be stuck.

Why can't she add the second master catalogue to the list of catalogues it contains within its pages?

(SOLUTION ON PAGE 121)

QUICKIE 13

Your bedroom clock is broken.
Every hour it gains thirty-six minutes.
However, exactly one hour ago it stopped, showing
the time as eight twenty-four A.M. You know that it
showed the right time at two A.M.

What time is it now?

(SOLUTIONS ON PAGE 140)

QUICKIE 14

A group of fifty soldiers suffered
the following injuries in battle:
thirty-six soldiers lost an eye,
thirty-five lost an ear,
forty lost a leg, and forty-two lost an arm.

*What is the minimum number
of soldiers who must have lost all four?*

THE LIAR'S PARADOX

Baron Münchhausen prides himself on always being able to tell whether a statement is true or false. He insists, for example, that he was the first person to realize that Hannibal was being less than forthcoming with the truth when he stated that he was acquiring elephants with a view to entering the circus business.

Münchhausen is somewhat perturbed then to receive a telephone call from a fellow calling himself Eubulides, who claims that there are some statements where Münchhausen won't even know how to get started working out whether they are true or false. Münchhausen is not the kind of man to turn down the chance to outsmart a long-dead philosopher, so he challenges Eubulides to make good his claim.

Eubulides offers up the following sentence as an opening gambit:

> This sentence is false.

Münchhausen immediately sees the problem. If the sentence is true, then what it asserts is true, but what it asserts is that it is false, which means that it must be false. But if it is false, then what it asserts is false, but what it asserts is that it is false, which means that it must be true. This is surely paradoxical. Münchhausen takes a deep breath, and resisting the temptation to cry, offers his rejoinder: the truth of this particular sentence is that it is neither true nor false; not every proposition has to be either true or false.

Münchhausen congratulates himself on a neat save but, unfortunately for him, Eubulides is not finished yet. He offers up the following sentence:

> This statement is not true.

Münchhausen thinks for a moment, and realizes that he is in big trouble. He can no longer claim that the statement is neither true nor false, and he cannot see how he can escape the paradox.

Is Münchhausen right to think that this statement cannot be neither true nor false, and if so, why? Is there any other way for him to escape the paradox?

(SOLUTION ON PAGE 122)

ST. PETERSBURG PARADOX

George McClellan, a cabaret performer at the renowned Hotel Infinity, is intrigued to see that its casino is promoting a new game of chance, which it claims will make somebody very rich indeed. McClellan has a few hours to kill before his one man show—*A Dictator I Could Be*—is due to begin, so he decides to check out the game. He finds that it works as follows.

A fair coin is tossed until it lands tails up. If this happens on the first throw, the player gets $2, and the game ends; if it happens on the second throw, it's $4, and the game ends; on the third throw $8, and the game ends, and so on. In other words, the player will win $2 to the power of n, where n is the number of coin tosses it takes for the coin to land on tails.

However, there is a catch. Before every game, the casino holds an auction in which people bid to play the game. Only the person bidding the highest amount of money is able to take part. George McClellan is a rich man, but also risk-averse, so he calculates some probabilities to help him determine how much he should bid.

McClellan looks at the figures for a while and then remembers that he's a mime artist, not a statistician, so he calls his friend, the seemingly ubiquitous Inspector Horse, for some advice.

NUMBER OF TOSSES UNTIL A TAIL (N)	PROBABILITY OF N	PRIZE
1	1/2	$2
2	1/4	$4
3	1/8	$8
4	1/16	$16
5	1/32	$32
6	1/64	$64
7	1/128	$128
8	1/256	$256
9	1/512	$512
10	1/1024	$1024

How much money does Horse recommend that McClellan bid in order to take part in the game? And why?

(SOLUTION ON PAGE 124)

PARADOX OF THE COURT

As an undergraduate about to enter law school, Bailey Winepol put into action what he thought was the perfect scheme to avoid paying school fees. He managed to persuade Lock Haven Law to sign up for a deal that would contractually oblige him to pay double the normal school fees, but only when he won his first court case. Until then, he would be required to pay nothing. However, what the administrators at the law school did not know was that young Bailey only ever intended to take on cases that he could not possibly win.

Sure enough, this is precisely how his career has unfolded in the five years since he entered the Bar. Winepol has built up a successful business by means of the shrewd application of the following guiding philosophy: strive to take on only those clients who have committed their crimes live on national television and then signed a confession in front of millions of people.

Unfortunately for Winepol, a new face has recently taken over the reins at Lock Haven Law, a Professor Protagoras, who is not prepared to tolerate these shenanigans any longer. The Professor has come up with a plan every bit as devious as Winepol's in order to get him to cough up the money. He decides to sue Winepol in court for the money he owes.

Protagoras doesn't expect the law school to win the case, but he believes that it will end up getting its money anyway. He reasons as follows: if Winepol wins, then he will have won his first case, which means that he will be obliged to pay the amount he owes. If he doesn't win, then it means that the court has confirmed that he has to pay the money. Either way, Lock Haven Law gets paid.

Winepol, needless to say, doesn't see it quite like this. He believes that if he wins the case, it means the court has determined that he doesn't have to pay the money. If he loses, he has still not won his first case, which means that he is not obliged to pay. So either way, the law school does not get paid.

Which of the two of them has got it right?
And why?

(SOLUTION ON PAGE 127)

BURIDAN'S ASS

Hector House is on trial at Lesser Bovey crown court. His attempt to steal a pedigree tortoise from a marina went wrong after the recalcitrant reptile escaped and sprinted off. House had ended up brawling with his partner in crime, Arthur Achilles, who then ratted him out to the police as part of a plea bargain.

House has no choice but to admit to the attempted theft, but makes the following submission to the jury in an attempt to avoid jail.

Jury Members,

It is true that I attempted to procure a pedigree tortoise via illicit means. However, I should not be punished for my crimes. Human beings are mere complicated machines, and like any machine, our behavior is inexorably determined by mechanistic processes. My crimes were the inevitable outcome of prior events in my life, which themselves were the effects of earlier prior events, and so on, all the way back to my birth. I was always going to attempt to steal a tortoise, because human beings cannot but act in the way that they do actually act. Therefore, I am not responsible for what happened, and I should be found not guilty.

Unfortunately for House, the prosecuting council has secured Inspector Horse as an expert witness to counter this defence. The Inspector asks the jury to consider the following scenario.

A hungry donkey is standing precisely between two identical bales of hay. There is nothing in the situation, nor in the donkey's past, that could lead him to favor one bale of hay over the other. Therefore, if causal determinism is true— as House suggests—the donkey will be unable to choose between the two bales of hay. He will simply stand there trapped in indecision until he starves to death. It is just about possible to imagine that this might happen to a donkey. However, it is surely the case that a human being in this situation would make a choice rather than starve. This means that causal determinism cannot be true for human beings. We must have free will. Therefore, Hector House's defence fails, and he should be found guilty of his crimes.

Is Inspector Horse right? Does the fact that a human being will choose in this situation mean that free will exists?

(SOLUTION ON PAGE 128)

6

PARADOXICAL ALL THE WAY DOWN

How wonderful that we have met with a paradox.
Now we have some hope of making progress.
NIELS BOHR: *ATTRIBUTED*

A genuine paradox has the following form: a premise (or premises) that will be accepted as being true by most right-thinking people; an argument from premises to conclusion that seemingly obeys all the normal rules of logic; but crucially, a conclusion that is apparently unthinkable. The Sorites Paradox, which appears in Chapter 4, perfectly exhibits this form:

PREMISE: A person with 10,000 hairs is not bald.
ARGUMENT: Subtracting one hair from any number of hairs cannot make the difference between a person being not bald and being bald.
CONCLUSION: A person with no hair is not bald?

Normally, the way to solve a paradox is to show either that there is something wrong with the premise(s), or that there is something wrong with the argument. However, as I'm sure you've discovered, or will discover whilst working through this book, this is not always very easy to do. In fact, sometimes it proves to be so difficult that the sensible conclusion is that what we're confronted with is a paradox all the way down.

NEWCOMB'S PARADOX

Frosty Reading is visiting Rockhampton Clairvoyants Inc., the world's most accurate prediction agency, with the expectation of hearing some news about the (he hopes) imminent demise of his next door neighbor, whose house he covets. Frosty is rather taken aback to find that his personal consultation has been cancelled—due to entirely foreseen circumstances—and that instead he has been asked to play a game that should net him a very large sum of money.

The nature of the game is explained to Frosty as follows. He will be presented with two opaque boxes: Box A will contain $10,000; and Box B will contain $1,000,000 or nothing. He will then be given the choice between taking home both boxes or taking only Box B.

Frosty is told that the amount of money in Box B will be determined by Rockhampton's most accurate clairvoyant—for all intents and purposes, 100 percent accurate—on the following basis. If the psychic predicts that Frosty will take home both boxes, then no money will be put into Box B. If she predicts that he will take home only Box B, then $1,000,000 will be placed into the box. The prediction will

already have been made by the time the game starts, and the amount of money in Box B already fixed.

The philosopher Robert Nozick said of this game that everybody thinks it is perfectly clear and obvious what should be done, but that one half think one thing, and the other half another, and both groups tend to think the other group is just daft.

So should Frosty Reading take both boxes or just Box B?

(SOLUTION ON PAGE 130)

TIPS TO GET YOU STARTED

PREDICTED CHOICE	ACTUAL CHOICE	BOX A PAYOUT	BOX B PAYOUT	TOTAL PAYOUT
BOX A&B	BOX A&B	$10,000	$0	$10,000
BOX A&B	BOX B	$10,000	$0	$0
BOX B	BOX A&B	$10,000	$1,000,000	$1,010,000
BOX B	BOX B	$0	$1,000,000	$1,000,000

THE SURPRISE PARTY

Clare Brogan embraced misanthropy at an early age. Even as a toddler, she could be found standing on a crate at Speaker's Corner denouncing humanity.

She is none too pleased then when, a week before her 18th birthday, her parents, who are scrupulously reliable, announce that they are throwing a surprise birthday party for her, complete with a virtuoso clown performance. Clare is at first horrified, but then she starts to think about precisely what her parents have promised, and realizes that she has nothing to worry about. The party is not going to take place.

Her reasoning is that as her parents stated that the party would happen on a weekday the following week, and that it would come as a surprise, then it cannot happen on the Friday, because if it hasn't happened by midnight on Thursday, she will know it has to happen on Friday, which means that it won't be a surprise. But it follows then that it also cannot happen on Thursday, since if it hasn't happened by midnight on Wednesday, she will know that it has to happen on Thursday (since it can't happen on Friday), which again means that it won't be a surprise. This reasoning works for all the days backwards through the week, which leads Clare to conclude that the party cannot take place.

Is Clare right to think that the surprise party will not take place?

(SOLUTION ON PAGE 132)

QUICKIE 15

A boy and a girl are sitting together on a park bench.
"I'm a girl," says the child with blonde hair.
"I'm a boy," says the child with brown hair.
At least one of them is lying.

Which child is the girl, and which the boy?

(SOLUTIONS ON PAGE 141)

QUICKIE 16

A farmer has to cross a river in a boat.
He has a chicken, a fox, and a bag of grain with him.
The boat is only big enough for him to take one
of the three across at a time. He cannot leave the grain
and the chicken alone together, since the chicken will
eat the grain. And he cannot leave the fox and chicken
alone together, since the fox will eat the chicken.

How does he get everything
safely across the river?

THE LOTTERY PARADOX

Alex Gibbon, a sociologist at North Bovey Institute of Technology, is keen to tell anybody who will listen that he doesn't like Lotto, his country's national lottery competition. If he goes to a party, he inevitably feels morally bound to offer an impromptu lecture on what he calls the lottery tax, explaining also that big prize lotteries are the new opium of the people, designed to dissolve the revolutionary fervor of the masses by holding out the promise of riches beyond imagination.

Professor Gibbon, though, has an embarrassing secret. Every week, he buys a lottery ticket. He tells himself that he does so out of solidarity with working people. If he thought that he might win, then he wouldn't buy the ticket. Happily, the chances that any single ticket will win are so unlikely—some 14 million to 1—that he could buy a ticket every week for a quarter of million years before expecting to win. Admittedly, he watches the Lotto draw on television, but really this is only so that he can fully appreciate the ideological force of the whole charade.

Gibbon carries on happily in this way for many years until he foolishly confesses his lottery secret to a colleague in the philosophy department at NBIT. The philosopher responds that Gibbon cannot really believe that his ticket is going to lose each week. He explains why as follows. The probability that any individual ticket will win the lottery is incredibly unlikely. Therefore, if somebody has ticket number 234,456, for example, it is rational to believe that it will not be the winning ticket. It follows, that it is also rational to believe that no other particular ticket will be the winner. However, this means that it is also rational to believe that no ticket will win the lottery, yet we know that (normally) some ticket will win. Therefore, we have a contradiction: we think both that no particular ticket will win and yet that a ticket will win.

The philosopher tells Professor Gibbon that the only way he can escape this contradiction is to believe that his ticket might win.

Is the philosopher right? Must Gibbon concede that he might end up rich beyond his wildest dreams?

(SOLUTION ON PAGE 133)

THE SLEEPING BEAUTY PROBLEM

Sleeping Beauty has been experiencing a little local difficulty with her rather slothful Prince Charming. It turns out that he has expensive tastes in fine jewelry and croissants, which means that the money she earns from her job in narcolepsy research is not covering her outgoings. A concerned Sleeping Beauty decides to earn a little extra pocket money so that she can spoil him still further. To this end, she signs up to take part in a research procedure that has the following form.

On Sunday, Sleeping Beauty will be given a drug that puts her to sleep. A fair coin will be flipped. If it comes up heads, she will be awakened on Monday, then questioned, and the experiment ends. If it comes up tails, she will be awakened on Monday, questioned, and then given another dose of the sleeping drug. She will then be awakened again on Tuesday, after which the experiment will end. Although Sleeping Beauty has been told all the details of the experiment, she has no way of knowing, before or during her questioning, what day of the week it is. The sleeping drug also induces mild memory loss, so she knows that she will not be able to remember any previous awakenings during the experiment (if there are any).

During her questioning, she is asked one thing:

> What is her estimate of the probability that the
> coin came up heads? Or to put this another way,
> how much confidence does she have that the coin
> came up heads?

There are two factors to take into account when considering this question. First, the fact that the course that the experiment takes—whether there are one or two awakenings—is determined by a single toss of a fair coin. And second, the pattern of Sleeping Beauty's awakenings: one awakening if the coin comes up heads, two if it comes up tails.

How should Sleeping Beauty answer the question?

(SOLUTION ON PAGE 134)

QUICKIE 17

The following people were at a family reunion:
one grandfather,
one grandmother,
two fathers,
two mothers,
four children,
three grandchildren,
two sisters,
one brother,
two daughters,
two sons,
one father-in-law,
one mother-in-law,
and one daughter-in-law.

*What's the fewest number of people
who could have attended the reunion,
and who were they?*

QUICKIE 18

*Is it legal for a man in Belgium
to marry his widow's sister?*

(SOLUTIONS ON PAGE 141)

QUICKIE 19

You have ten sets of ten weights. You know how much the weights should weigh. You also know that all the weights in one set are one kilogram out, which means that the weight of the entire faulty set is ten kilograms out. You further know that the fault only occurs in one set. You are allowed to use an accurate weighing machine just once.

*How do you work out which
set of weights is faulty?*

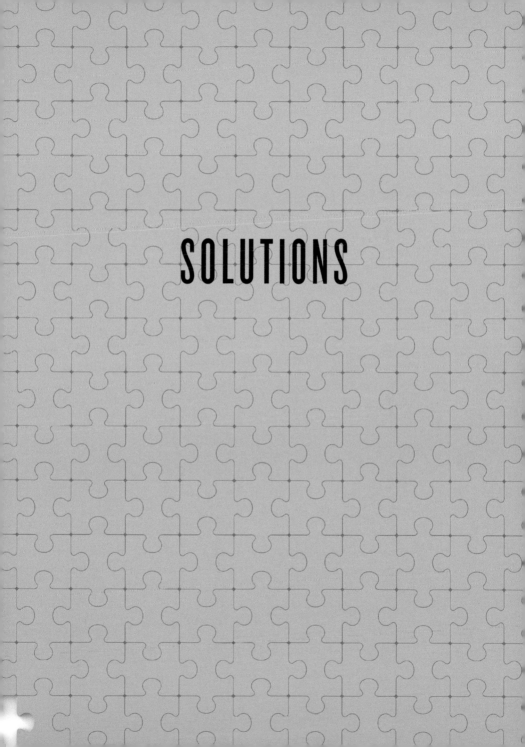

SOLUTIONS

EINSTEIN'S RIDDLE SOLUTION

- Fact # 14 combined with Fact #9 means that House 2 is blue.
- Fact # 4 together with Fact # 5 means that House 4 is green, coffee is consumed in House 4, and House 5 is white.
- Fact # 1 means that the British man lives in House 3, which is red. This means that House 1 is yellow (since yellow is the only color left). We also know that the person in the yellow house plays baseball (Fact # 7), and that the horse belongs to House 2, next to the baseball player (Fact # 11).
- Fact # 12 states that the owner who plays tennis also drinks beer. So what nationality is he? He can't be Norwegian (plays baseball) or British (drinks milk). He can't be German (Fact # 13) or Danish (Fact # 3). He must be Swedish. What do we know about the Swedish man? Fact # 2 tells us he keeps dogs. Therefore, we know the Swedish man plays tennis, drinks beer, and keeps dogs. This will only fit in House 5.
- Fact # 3 now tells us that the Danish man must be in House 2, and that the person who drinks tea is also in House 2. This means that the water drinker must be in House 1, and the German in House 4.
- Fact # 15 means that the person who plays volleyball must be in House 2, and Fact # 13 means that the person who plays hockey is in House 4. This in turn means that the football player is in House 3, and we also know that he rears birds (Fact # 6)
- Fact # 10 gives us cats for House 1.

Now we have our answer:

The fish is owned by the German who lives in green House 4, drinks coffee, and plays hockey!

	HOUSE 1	HOUSE 2	HOUSE 3	HOUSE 4	HOUSE 5
NATIONALITY	Norwegian	Danish	British	German	Swedish
COLOR	yellow	blue	red	green	white
BEVERAGE	water	tea	milk	coffee	beer
SPORT	baseball	volleyball	football	hockey	tennis
PET	cats	horse	birds	FISH!	dogs

FERARRI OR GOAT SOLUTION

William Capra is struggling with what is known as the Monty Hall problem. At first sight, almost everybody thinks that there is no advantage in switching to a new door. Presumably, they reason that there is an equal chance of the car being behind any of the doors, so choosing a new door isn't going to make any difference. This is wrong.

William should switch doors. If you switch, the only circumstance in which you don't win the car is if you originally picked the door with the car behind it. After you make your original choice, the quiz master must open a door with a goat behind it (because doing otherwise would reveal the car). Therefore, if you originally chose a door with a goat behind it, he is forced to reveal the only remaining goat to you, thereby telling you which door has the car behind it (the door he hasn't opened). The chance that you originally chose a door with a goat is 2 in 3. This means that by switching you have a 2 in 3 chance of winning, which is better than the original 1 in 3 chance of winning.

If this is confusing, the following diagram will help to show the various possibilities:

(SEE DIAGRAM ON PAGE 88-89)

The diagram makes it clear that if you first chose the car then you lose if you switch; but if you first chose either of the goats, then you win by switching. There is a probability of 2/3 that you chose a goat to start with (scenario 2 and 3). Therefore, you should switch, since this means that 2 times out of 3 you will win.

After Marilyn vos Savant featured the problem in *Parade*, she received the following missive from University of Florida professor Charles Reid:

"May I suggest that you obtain and refer to a standard textbook on probability before you try to answer a question of this type again?"

Vos Savant's response was to explain again why her solution was correct, and to ask her readers to conduct the experiment at home for themselves. This they did in their thousands, with their results confirming, as she had stated, that you win twice as often if you change your original choice.

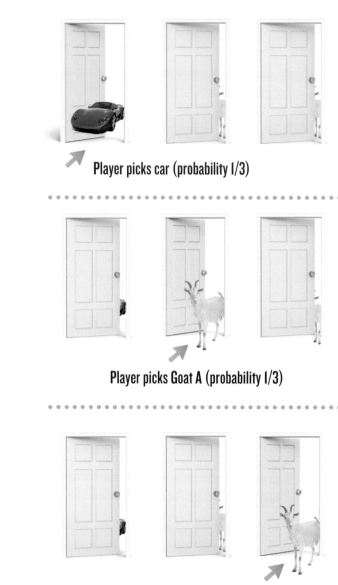

1.

Player picks car (probability 1/3)

2.

Player picks Goat A (probability 1/3)

3.

Player picks Goat B (probability 1/3)

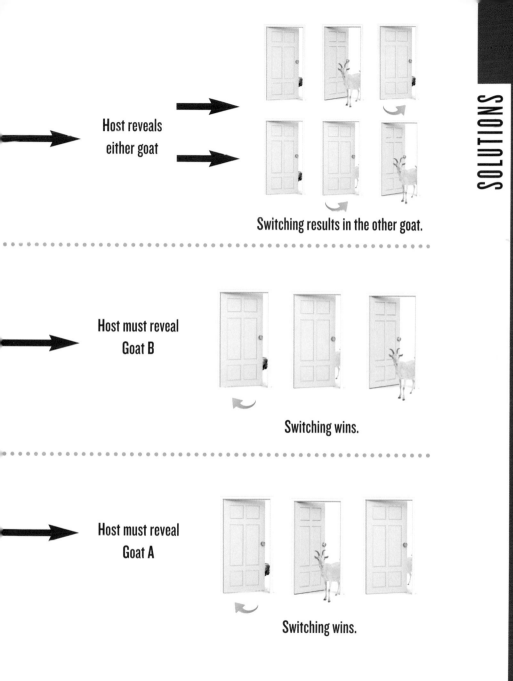

Host reveals
either goat

Switching results in the other goat.

Host must reveal
Goat B

Switching wins.

Host must reveal
Goat A

Switching wins.

BERTRAND'S BOX SOLUTION

This is a version of a puzzle that was originally posed in the nineteenth century by the French mathematician Joseph Bertrand. The key to solving it is to imagine that the initial selection is among six possible drawers (not three possible caskets). Thus:

Casket 1	Pearl	Pearl
Casket 2	Pearl	Coal
Casket 3	Coal	Coal

There are three drawers that contain a pearl, each with an equal chance of being chosen (a probability of one-third). One of these drawers is in Casket 2, so the probability that Iowa Jones chose a drawer from Casket 2 is one-third. Two of the drawers are in Casket 1, which means that the probability that he chose a drawer from Casket 1, and that he will find another pearl when he breaks open the second drawer, is two-thirds.

People overwhelmingly tend to get this puzzle wrong. This is normally because they think in terms of caskets rather than drawers. In this case, they would reason that since Iowa Jones cannot have opened Casket 3, he must have opened either Casket 1 or Casket 2, which means that there must be a probability of one-half that the second unopened drawer will contain a pearl—if he opened Casket 1, it will, if Casket 2, it won't.

However, the reality is that Dr. Jones chose a drawer not a casket, which leaves three possibilities:

1. He chose the Pearl of Pearl-Coal, and the other drawer contains the coal (1/3).
2. He chose Pearl 1 of Pearl-Pearl, and the other drawer contains a Pearl (1/3).
3. He chose Pearl 2 of Pearl-Pearl, and the other drawer contains a Pearl (1/3).

Thus, it follows that there is a probability of two-thirds that Iowa Jones will find a pearl in the second drawer rather than a lump of coal.

BOY OR GIRL SOLUTION

The chances are that you think that Martin has got this wrong. Probably, you reason that since there is a 50 percent probability that any particular child is a boy or a girl, it must be equally likely that Martin's other child is a boy or a girl. If so, then you've gone wrong. In fact, the probability that Martin's second child is a girl is two-thirds.

This is because, for a family with two children, there are four possible combinations (with the younger child first):

Girl - Girl
Girl - Boy
Boy - Girl
Boy - Boy

In Martin's situation, we know that at least one of his two children is a boy. This rules out the possibility that both his children are girls. So we are left with three possible combinations of children:

Younger Child	Older Child
Girl	Boy
Boy	Girl
Boy	Boy

This shows that there is a girl in two of the three possible combinations that remain. Therefore, the probability that Martin has a daughter as well as a son is two-thirds (and the probability that he has two sons—that is, that his other child is a boy—is one-third).

It is possible that you think that there's something wrong here in that the Boy-Boy combination counts only once. However, closer examination reveals that in fact Boy-Boy represents only one possibility:

BOY-BOY[1] — there is a younger boy who has an older brother describes exactly the same thing as:
BOY-BOY[2] — there is an older boy who has a younger brother.

In contrast, the Girl-Boy and Boy-Girl combinations represent two separate possibilities:

GIRL-BOY — there is a younger girl who has an older brother.
BOY-GIRL — there is an older girl who has a younger brother.

It follows, then, that there is a two-thirds probability that there is a girl in the family, and only a one-third probability that there are two boys.

HOW OLD ARE THEY? SOLUTION

This is a version of a puzzle that appeared in *Popular Science* magazine in April 1960. It is a straightforward logic puzzle: there are no tricks to it, solving it is just a matter of reasoning correctly.

We should start with what we know: namely, that if we multiply together the ages of the three people living in the house we'll get the figure 225. To work out which permutations of ages this is true of, it is necessary to determine the factors of 225 (i.e., the whole numbers which when multiplied together equal 225).

I x 225 = 225

3 x 75 = 225

5 x 45 = 225

9 x 25 = 225

15 x 15 = 225

giving us factors I, 3, 5, 9, I5, 25, 45, 75, 225

From these factors, it is possible to derive eight permutations of ages which when multiplied together equal 225. This also gives us the possible house numbers (the sum of the ages of the people living in the house).

We now have enough information to work out the ages of the people living in the house. It will be remembered that Inspector Horse commanded Gibbon to ask an additional question about the girl's age compared to her siblings. Horse, as well as Gibbon, knows the number of the house, so the

Person 1 Age	Person 2 Age	Person 3 Age	House Number
225	1	1	227
75	3	1	79
45	5	1	51
25	9	1	35
25	3	3	31
15	15	1	31
15	5	3	23
9	5	1	15

only reason he needs this further information is because there is more than one combination of ages to which the house number is equal. This rules out every house number except 31.

There are two possible combinations of ages of people living at house number 31: 25, 3, 3 or 15, 15, 1.

The answer to the question that Gibbon asked—"Are you much older than your siblings?"—gives us the correct ages. The woman at the door answered "Yes," which rules out 15, 15, and 1 as an option.

This means that the people living in the house must be 25, 3, and 3.

ELEMENTARY, MY DEAR WASON SOLUTION

The test that Officer Dawe was required to take—devised by psychologist Peter Wason some forty years ago—is more than just the kind of conundrum you tend to find in a puzzle book. It tells us something about the way that our reasoning ability is structured, and in particular whether we are any good at detecting violations of conditional rules (that is, rules of the nature "If x, then y").

The correct answer is that it is necessary to turn over two cards in order to determine whether the rule that states that if a card has a circle on one side then it has the color yellow on the other has been upheld. These cards are: the circle and the color red.

This is the logic:

- The square does not have to be turned over since it doesn't matter what color is on the other side (because the rule says nothing about the color that squares have to be paired with).

- The circle has to be turned over, since the other side might not be yellow, which would break the rule.

- The yellow does not have to be turned over because it doesn't matter what shape is on the other side—the rule did not say that yellow must only ever be paired with a circle, it just said that if you've got a circle then you've got to have yellow on the other side.

- Red has to be turned over, since there might be a circle on the other side, which would break the rule.

As we have noted, we are terribly bad at this kind of test, so the chances are that you got it wrong. If so, don't worry too much, though perhaps there is reason for some pause for thought. There is a common idea that our beliefs about the world should be logically coherent—at least in some sense based on sound reasoning. However, if we systematically and unconsciously reason badly, then it must be questionable whether this is the case.

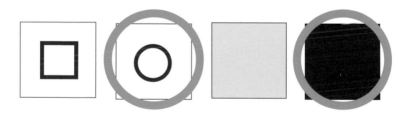

WHAT DOES MARY DO? SOLUTION

When asked to judge what Mary is likely to be doing with her life, most people estimate that it is more likely that she is a bank clerk and active in the feminist movement (statement 4) than that she is a bank clerk (statement 2). However, this is a logical mistake, and clearly impossible. If Mary is a bank clerk and a feminist, then she is a bank clerk. In other words, Mary cannot be a bank clerk and a feminist without being a bank clerk, so the former can't be more likely than the latter.

This basic logical error can also be expressed as follows: the probability that someone or something fulfils a conjunction of two properties (i.e., being a bank clerk and a feminist) cannot be greater than the probability that they fulfil just one of them (in this instance, only being a bank clerk).

There is something a little bit shocking about the fact that people tend to go wrong here. After all, it does seem a rather obvious mistake. So what's the explanation? What is most likely is that we're being misled here by conversational expectations. Put simply, when we have to choose between a series of options, which includes "Mary is a bank clerk" and "Mary is a bank clerk and active in the feminist movement," we assume that the absence of any mention of feminism in the first option is equivalent to claiming that "Mary is a bank clerk and *not active in the feminist movement.*" If that's the case, then we're being led by conversational expectations towards an answer that is formally incorrect.

Even if this is the explanation for our tendency to get this kind of reasoning wrong, everyday errors like this provide a salutary lesson. It seems that we're not nearly as logical as we'd like to suppose.

THE GAMBLER'S MISTAKE SOLUTION

Karen has realized that she has fallen for a trick that relies on the laws of probability, simple division, and the vagaries of human psychology for its effect.

Here's how it works:

Soccer Predictions Ltd purchases a mailing list with a million e-mail addresses on it. The company then sends out its first e-mail. Half the people on the list get an e-mail saying that Derby County will win; the other half get an e-mail saying their opponents will win (we'll assume for the purposes of illustration that all matches end in a victory for one side). This means that whatever the outcome of the game, 500,000 people will have received a correct prediction. These people, and only these people, then get another e-mail predicting the outcome of a further match. Half of them are told that one team will win; the other half, that the other team will win. At the end of this process, there will be some number of people who have received only correct predictions. It seems to them that Soccer Predictions Ltd has correctly predicted the result of every game. However, the reality is that the company has predicted all possible results: it just happens that people such as Karen have received the single set of entirely correct predictions.

So what Karen worked out was that almost certainly she was not the only person receiving these e-mails, and that the set of people who had received an incorrect prediction was likely incomparably larger than the set of people who had received only correct predictions.

THE THIEVING CLOWN SOLUTION

Imagine Bozo College is a thieves' paradise and there have been a hundred thefts there in the recent past, all of them perpetrated by trainee clowns. There is an equal probability that any particular clown will be a thief. It follows that we'd expect eighty-five of the thefts to have been perpetrated by clowns with blue noses and fifteen by clowns with red noses.

Now consider the witness reports. There are four possibilities here:

(1) blue-nosed clown guilty, witness correctly reports blue nose (with 80% probability)

(2) blue-nosed clown guilty, witness incorrectly reports red nose (with 20% probability)

(3) red-nosed clown guilty, witness correctly reports red nose (with 80% probability)

(4) red-nosed clown guilty, witness incorrectly reports blue nose (with 20% probability).

Now the problem becomes quite easy to solve. In order to determine the probability that the thief had a red nose, we need to know how often a witness reports that a red-nosed clown is the perpetrator, and on how many of these occasions a red-nosed clown is actually the perpetrator. A simple table will help us work this out.

	BLUE-NOSED CLOWN IS THIEF	RED-NOSED CLOWN IS THIEF
NUMBER OF ACTUAL CASES	85	15
WITNESS REPORTS: BLUE NOSE RED NOSE	68 = 80% OF 85 17 = 20% OF 85	3 = 20% OF 15 12 = 80% OF 15

This tells us that on twenty-nine separate occasions a witness will identify the thief as having a red nose (17 + 12). However, on only twelve of these occasions will the thief actually have had a red nose (on the other seventeen occasions the witness will have misidentified a blue-nosed clown as having a red nose).

The answer therefore is that there is a 41 percent probability (12/29) that the thief at Bozo College had a red nose. Many people find this answer surprising. They assume that because witnesses are right 80 percent of the time then there is an 80 percent chance that a red-nosed clown is the thief. However, this assumption fails to take into account the large number of occasions that witnesses will misidentify a blue-nosed thief as having a red nose.

THE DISAPPEARING DOLLAR SOLUTION

In a sense, the solution to this trick is easy. The key to working out what has gone wrong here is to look for the misdirection in the description of what has occurred. The conundrum works because, like a good magic trick, it dupes people into accepting something that isn't true.

It is true that each salesman has paid $9 towards their room—in other words, that they have paid $27 in total. However, this $27 *includes* the $2 that the bellboy has pocketed, so there is no extra $2 to add to $27 to make $29. The $30 is a red herring: this is what the salesmen originally paid, but it is out of the equation once the $3 has been paid back to them.

To make all this clear, consider the following:

Salesmen pay $30 for room.	Hotel has $30.
Manager gives bellboy $5 out of this $30.	Hotel has $25. Bellboy has $5.
Bellboy returns $3 to Salesmen	Hotel has $25. Bellboy has $2. (Salesmen have $3)
Salesmen have paid $27 dollars in total.	Hotel has $25. Bellboy has $2.

This shows that of the $27 paid by the salesmen, $25 has gone to the hotel, and $2 has gone to the bellboy, so there is no logical reason to add the bellboy's $2 to the salesmen's $27 (which already includes the bell boy's $2).

The conundrum works because people are misled by a misdirection that occurs in the original description of what has happened. They think along the lines of, "So we've got the $27 that the salesmen have paid (3 x $9); and the $2 that the bellboy has pocketed."

No we don't. We have the $27 that the salesmen have paid, which includes the $2 that the bellboy has pocketed.

THE PRISONER'S DILEMMA SOLUTION

There is no right answer, as such, to the Prisoner's Dilemma. However, if a prisoner in this situation wishes to maximize their own rewards—by gaining as small a prison sentence as possible—then they should always betray their associate.

For example, Arthur can reason as follows:

It is possible that Hector will remain silent, but if he does, and I betray him, I'll go free (and Hector will get ten years in jail). The other possibility is that he'll talk, but if he does, and I don't betray him, I'll go to jail for ten years, and he'll go free. Therefore, I will always be better off by betraying him.

The trouble is, of course, Hector can reason in exactly the same way, and it is this that produces the dilemma. Arthur and Hector both act in their own best interest by betraying the other, but, as a result, they end up worse off than they would have done had they acted less than maximally by keeping quiet.

It is possible you're thinking that this shows that the most rational strategy is the cooperative strategy of keeping quiet. After all, it seems counterintuitive to suppose that a strategy that leads to a worse outcome (betraying) could be more rational than one that will lead to a better outcome (keeping quiet).

However, the significant point is that the cooperative strategy is not the best strategy for any individual prisoner in this situation. Consider, for example, that Arthur might reason about the cooperative strategy as follows:

> Hector is smart enough to realize that if we both act in our own best interest then we'll both end up in prison. Therefore, he'll choose the cooperative strategy of keeping quiet. So perhaps I should keep quiet, too? Except, if Hector does indeed keep quiet, then I stand to lose nothing by not keeping quiet, and I stand to gain my freedom if I betray him. So it makes no sense for me not to talk.

There is one caveat here. If people are actually put into this kind of situation, and given these kinds of choices, there is evidence that a large minority of them will choose the cooperative strategy even though it is the less rational strategy. However, this may be evidence of our inability to reason properly rather than our trusting nature!

THE DOLLAR AUCTION SOLUTION

The dollar auction scenario was originally devised by the economist Martin Shubik. It is designed to show that seemingly irrational behavior can result from a series of perfectly rational steps. It works because once two bids have been placed, it almost always pays the second-highest bidder to beat the current highest bid. However, the consequence of this is that the overall position of the second-highest bidder gets worse and worse. Shubik reports that bids of three dollars and more are not uncommon if the auction is held for real.

Is there a way to outfox the auctioneer? Certainly it is possible for the auctioneer to lose, for example, if a one-cent bid is made, and no further bids are received. However, there is no sure way for a bidder to win the auction (assuming that he is not able to control the other bidders). His best chance to end the auction is to bid 99 cents more than the preceding bid, which will mean that the second-highest bidder stands to gain nothing by placing a further bid. (For example, if Bidder 1 bids 50 cents, and then Bidder 2 bids $1.49, Bidder 1 stands to lose 50 cents if he doesn't bid, and to lose 50 cents if he bets and wins the auction—the $1.50 he pays minus the $1.00 he wins. In other words, he gains nothing by continuing the auction.) The winning bidder still can't make a profit, but can at least bring the auction to an end before his losses get out of hand.

The difficulty is the fact that the second-highest bidder makes no financial gain by bidding does not mean that they will not bid. Part of the point of this situation is precisely that irrational impulses tend to come into play once people are involved in this kind of escalation war. It is entirely possible that Ronald Plump will amass a fortune, dollar by dollar.

THE GAMBLER'S FALLACY SOLUTION

Bobby de Faro's plan to scam his local Super Casino is a sure-fire loser. The first element of the plan is a classic example of what is known as the gambler's fallacy. This is the false belief that the chance that something with a fixed probability will occur increases or decreases depending on whether it has occurred in the recent past. The classic way of illustrating this is by the example of a series of coin tosses.

The probability that a fair coin will land on heads six times in a row is 1 in 64. Therefore, a gambler might think that if a coin has come up heads five time in a row, there is a 1 in 64 chance that it will land on heads on the sixth occasion. This is false. By definition, the probability that a fair coin will land on heads is always 50-50. The coin has no memory of what has occurred previously; it is simply irrelevant in terms of future probabilities that it has previously come up heads five times in a row. The same is true of a (fair) roulette table. De Faro is mistaken to suppose that the fact that there has been a run on one color says anything about what is going to happen next.

The second element of his plan is flawed for a related reason. The strategy of doubling every losing bet so that the first win recoups all prior losses, plus turns in a profit, is known as the Martindale betting system. In principle it is sound. However, the trouble with it is that the exponential growth of the value of bets required to cover a losing run will almost inevitably bankrupt the gambler who employs it. De Faro will find out the hard way that the fact that a roulette table has come up red four times in a row does not decrease the chance that it will come up red the next time.

LIES, DAMNED LIES, AND STATISTICS SOLUTION

The Mayor changed her mind in the case of Jim and Jules after Inspector Horse's suggestion that it might be interesting to combine the results from the games played against the two rival villages. She was rather staggered to find that despite the fact that Jim's average is better than Jules' against both villages, the overall average shows Jules outscoring Jim.

	JIM	JULES
GAMES PLAYED	14	16
TOTAL SCORE	820	970
AVERAGE	58.60	60.60

Inspector Horse explains that this has occurred because of something called Simpson's Paradox, which refers to those instances where combining small data sets into a larger data set produces a result that is seemingly the reverse of the result indicated by the smaller data sets (hence it is sometimes called the reversal paradox).

To understand how this has happened in the case of Jim and Jules, it is necessary only to recognize that Jules has played many more of the high-scoring games than Jim. This has had the effect of pushing his overall score upward relative to Jim's (even though in those few games Jim did play against Chudleigh-by-the-Ocean he scored better than Jules).

If this is still not clear, try calculating the combined scores on the basis of these figures (which still show Jim outperforming Jules against both villages):

Opponent: Chudleigh-by-the-Lake

	JIM	JULES
GAMES PLAYED	100	1
TOTAL SCORE	150	1
AVERAGE	1.5	1

Opponent: Chudleigh-by-the-Ocean

	JIM	JULES
GAMES PLAYED	1	100
TOTAL SCORE	95	9200
AVERAGE	95	92

The combined scores show that Jules's overall average is a lot higher than Jim's simply because he has taken part in many more of the easier games.

Simpson's Paradox has real-world implications. In 1973, University of California, Berkeley was sued after data showed that women applying to graduate school were less likely to be admitted than men. However, closer examination showed that no such bias existed at the level of individual departments. The explanation for the overall figure was simply that many more women than men applied for entry into competitive programs, which tended to turn down most applicants. The lesson of Simpson's Paradox is that it is necessary to treat large data sets built out of multiple, smaller data sets with extreme caution.

THE PARADOX OF DETERRENCE SOLUTION

There is certainly some tension when it comes to the idea of deterrence. However, in the case of Stanley Love's pumpkins, it is not insoluble. His thought process follows the line that there is nothing to justify harming the Meddy Posse, since the offence that he is trying to deter has already taken place.

However, it is at least arguable that retaliation against the Posse is justified to the extent that it would then deter *future* incidents involving his pumpkins. In other words, the deterrent effect will be reinforced into the future if he acts as the signs around his property state he will act. (Of course, this is not to justify the particular form of his deterrent, nor is it to suggest that acting in such a way would necessarily be legal!)

Nevertheless, there is something in the thought that in certain circumstances the idea of a deterrent is paradoxical. For example, imagine that you're the leader of a nation confronting a hostile power that has a much bigger army and

vastly superior conventional weapons to your own. You might rely on a nuclear deterrent for your own security. However, you know that if the deterrent fails (i.e. if the hostile power launches an attack against you anyway) there is absolutely no point in carrying out the retaliation that constitutes the deterrent (i.e., launching your weapons). You cannot win a war by following such a course of action; in fact, all you're going to do is cause the deaths of millions of people.

However, if you know beforehand that you will not or should not respond in the event of an attack, then you cannot form the sincere intention to retaliate that makes the deterrent work in the first place, and to this extent your security will be compromised.

This kind of thinking has led some people to flirt with the idea of creating a Doomsday machine that is programed—and cannot be unprogramed—to retaliate automatically in the event of an all-out attack rather than relying on a human who may shirk such action. However, as Dr. Strangelove discovered, a Doomsday machine can get you into trouble.

THE PARADOX OF JURISDICTION SOLUTION

It is likely that Judge Judy Solomon will conclude that there are no specific answers to the questions: Who killed Icarus? When was he killed? And where was he killed? This is not because there are no facts of the matter about what happened to the parrot, but rather because the questions are inappropriate. Specifically, they are an attempt to elicit information about the death of Icarus that does not exist. There are no further facts of the matter about what happened to the parrot other than that he was shot and wounded by Billy Blacklaw during a pheasant shoot in October, and then died the next spring in Lesser Bovey as a result of his wounds.

However, this conundrum is not without interest. Particularly, it has equivalents in the real world which will often require that some kind of decision about these matters is reached. The philosopher Alan Clark, for example, has pointed to a 1952 court case where it was determined that a defendant would be held liable for a defamatory radio program where it was heard, not where it was broadcast. Or consider that different states in the United States have different punishments for murder: some have the death penalty, some do not. It is quite easy to imagine a situation, analogous to the shooting of Icarus the parrot, where a court will have to determine under which jurisdiction a killer is to be held liable for his crime, and the decision that court makes could literally be the difference between life and death for the accused.

However, as Michael Clark points out in his study of this conundrum, even in this situation, the job of the court will not be to determine exactly when and where a killing took place, but rather simply to make a decision about liability. The court will not expand on the facts of the matter, just interpret what it already knows about an incident in terms of a particular legal framework.

BALD MAN LOGIC SOLUTION

Samson's argument that he will never be bald depends upon what is called the Sorites Paradox. The problem here is that it doesn't seem possible that taking one hair away from any number of hairs could ever make the difference between being "not bald" and "bald." "Bald" seems to be a vague concept that does not have sharp boundaries. However, the difficulty is that this premise entails a conclusion that is obviously false—at some point if you keep removing one hair, a person will be bald. We're left with a contradiction between what we know about the world (that if we remove Samson's hair, one strand at a time, he'll eventually be bald) and the conclusion of the argument (that he can never be bald). We have a bona fide paradox.

There is no generally agreed solution to the Sorites Paradox. However, there are many broad strategies for tackling it. One approach is to deny the premise that taking one hair away from a man who is not bald could never turn him into a bald man. This amounts to the claim that there is in fact a number of hairs for which subtracting one hair makes the difference between there being a non-bald head and a bald head. But this is highly counterintuitive. It seems to require what one philosopher called a "linguistic

miracle." After all, it just doesn't seem that a term such as "bald" has a precise definition.

An interesting facet of this paradox is that it has real-world implications. For example, consider the issue of how one determines the age at which a person is emotionally mature enough to have a sexual relationship. It is easy to imagine having an argument with a fifteen-year-old about whether they are old enough to have sex with their boyfriend, in which they say something like: "So, what you're claiming is that I will be mature enough to have sex on my sixteenth birthday, but I won't be mature enough to have sex the day before?" Or more trivially, consider that many people will think that it is acceptable to bring nine items to an eight items only checkout in a store, on the grounds that it really isn't worth worrying about an extra item. But if nine items are acceptable, and it isn't worth worrying about one extra item, it follows that ten items are acceptable, which means that eleven items must also be acceptable, and so on. If you find yourself flummoxed by the implications of such thoughts, then rest assured you're not alone, the Sorites Paradox has troubled philosophers for more than 2,000 years.

DOLLY'S CAT AND THE SHIP OF THESEUS SOLUTION

Dolly's fears about Montmorency's identity are related to a paradox traditionally known as the Ship of Theseus Paradox. It was originally stated by Plutarch as follows:

The ship wherein Theseus and the youth of Athens returned had thirty oars, and was preserved by the Athenians . . . they took away the old planks as they decayed, putting in new and stronger timber in their place, insomuch that this ship became a standing example among the philosophers, for the logical question of things that grow; one side holding that the ship remained the same, and the other contending that it was not the same.

Simply put, the paradox is that an object can be replaced piece by piece, until the point where nothing is left of the original, and yet it seems that it can still be the original object. Thus, in the case of Montmorency, most people's intuition is that the new Montmorency is the same cat as the old Montmorency, even though he is now made out of completely new material.

This sounds like a reasonable supposition, in which case Dolly needn't be too worried. Presumably it rests on the thought that Montmorency's identity is not defined by the *particular* elements that constitute his body, which means that it is not required that they endure across time. (Similarly, you probably do not think that your own personal identity requires that the various cells that make up your body are immortal.)

However, the paradox is not quite so simple to escape. Indeed, it isn't clear that it has a solution. For example, suppose that rather than throwing away Montmorency's old body parts, Dolly puts them into deep freeze. Then at a later point, she decides that she fancies having two furry companions, so reassembles the old Montmorency. In this situation, which cat is Montmorency? The temptation is to suppose that both cats are Montmorency, but this requires that we are committed to some version of the view that both cats are the same cat, which seems like a tall tale indeed.

HOTEL INFINITY SOLUTION

The problem of Hotel Infinity and the question of how many guests it can accommodate was first articulated by the mathematician David Hilbert. The solution to the version that appears here is actually reasonably straightforward, though in a sense it is highly counterintuitive.

In order to accommodate the infinite number of new guests, and to ensure that none of them end up in rooms already occupied, all that hotelier Basil Sinclair has to do is ask the existing guests to move rooms based on the following formula:

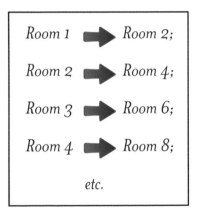

Room 1 ➡ *Room 2;*

Room 2 ➡ *Room 4;*

Room 3 ➡ *Room 6;*

Room 4 ➡ *Room 8;*

etc.

This will leave an infinite number of odd-numbered rooms free for the new guests. Once they have been checked in, every room in the hotel will be occupied again, but crucially, as Inspector Horse indicated, this does not mean

that there is no room for further guests. The hotelier can simply repeat this process, or some variation of it, in order to accommodate any new guests.

Although none of this is genuinely paradoxical, there is certainly some strangeness here. Consider, for example, that if half the guests now leave the hotel—perhaps all those occupying even-numbered rooms—it will be half-empty, yet still contain an infinite number of guests.

Perhaps you think that this problem was too easy to solve? If so, imagine a scenario where an infinite number of coaches arrives, each containing an infinite number of passengers. How would you accommodate all these new people whilst ensuring that they don't end up sharing rooms with each other?

ZENO AND THE THREE-LEGGED RACE SOLUTION

Achilles and the Tortoise is one of Zeno of Elea's classic paradoxes of motion, which seem to show that if space (and/or time) is infinitely divisible then motion is not possible at all. Consider, for example, that if you want to cross a room, then necessarily you must cover half the distance before you complete the journey. However, you can't cover half the distance until you cover half of half the distance, and you can't cover half of half the distance until you cover half of that distance, and so on, ad infinitum. It seems then that you'll never get started.

Of course, we know that people do cross rooms, and that a tortoise will get caught in a hundred meter sprint, which means that there must be something wrong with Zeno's argument. However, identifying exactly what is wrong is not easy. Perhaps the most popular approach is to argue that the paradox is dissolved by the fact that modern mathematics shows that an infinite series—$1/2 + 1/4 + 1/8 + 1/16 + \ldots$ has a finite sum, which means that there is some finite amount of time that it will take to traverse the series (how much time will depend upon distance and velocity).

However, this kind of response is just a little unsatisfying. As the philosopher Francis Moorcraft has pointed out, it seems almost to miss the point of Zeno's paradoxes. We already know that these do not pick out a feature of the real world. The interesting question is precisely where Zeno's reasoning goes wrong. We want to know what we say to the philosopher at the three-legged race when he asks us exactly where the argument fails, but this has been puzzling people for more than 2,000 years and there is no clear answer.

THE LIBRARIAN'S DILEMMA SOLUTION

Alexandra Pergamon, Cataloguer-in-Chief at the Lesser Bovey Library, has hit upon a real-world version of a paradox first uncovered by the philosopher Bertrand Russell. The issue she is wrestling with is whether a master catalogue which lists all those catalogues that do not contain a reference to themselves should contain a reference to itself. The problem is that if the catalogue does not contain a reference to itself, then it is a catalogue that does not contain a reference to itself, so it should contain a reference to itself (because it is cataloguing those catalogues that do not contain references to themselves). However, if it does contain a reference to itself, then it is not a catalogue that does not contain a reference to itself, in which case it should not contain a reference to itself. So she's stuck; there is a genuine paradox here.

This paradox can be expressed more formally as follows:

Does the set of all sets which don't include themselves as members, include itself as a member? If it does not, then it should; if it does, then it should not. Russell's paradox is (fairly) straightforward but its consequences were huge. It showed that there was something wrong with the way that people were thinking about logic and mathematics at the turn of the twentieth century.

There is an interesting side-story here. The paradox came to light in 1903 when Bertrand Russell sent a letter outlining it to the philosopher Gottlob Frege, who had spent thirty years of his life developing a theory of the foundations of mathematics. It is only a slight exaggeration to say that Frege's entire project was destroyed by this single letter.

THE LIAR'S PARADOX SOLUTION

Münchhausen has been wrestling with two versions of what is called the Liar's Paradox, first articulated by Eubulides of Miletus who lived in the fourth century B.C.E.

The sentence that has defeated him, *This statement is not true*, is known as the Strengthened Liar's Paradox. It is paradoxical because if false, then it is true (because its truth-claim is that it is false); but if true, then it is false (because the truth-claim is precisely that it is false). Moreover, Münchhausen is correct to think that he cannot respond that it is neither true nor false, because if it is neither true nor false, then it is not true, which is precisely what the statement asserts, thereby making it true, and leading one straight back into the paradox.

It might be some consolation to Münchhausen to know that there is no generally accepted way to escape this paradox. Probably the most common approach is to argue that statements that refer to themselves in this way are not properly meaningful. If this is right, then any paradoxes are dissolved, since the statements have no propositional content (that is, they make no claim that could be either true or false).

However, it is not clear that this is right. Francis Moorcroft has a neat illustration that makes this point. Imagine you find a card on the sidewalk, which on one side states:

> The sentence on the other side
> of this card is true.

And on the other side:

> The sentence on the other side
> of this card is false.

The difficulty here is that if the first sentence means nothing, why turn over the card to read the other side?

ST. PETERSBURG PARADOX SOLUTION

The solution to the question of the amount of money that George McClellan should bid is highly counterintuitive. Consequently, it is worth working it out in stages.

The first thing to determine is the expected value of the game—that is, how much a player would expect to win on average by playing the game. Consider the following simplified example, which features a game with two possible outcomes, both equally likely:

	PROBABILITY	PRIZE	EXPECTED PAYOFF (PRIZE DIVIDED BY PROBABILITY)
OUTCOME 1	50%	$2,000	$1,000
OUTCOME 2	50%	$200	$100
VALUE OF GAME			$1,100

This shows a game value of $1,100, which makes intuitive sense, since it is the average of the prizes of the two possible outcomes, both equally likely. The gambler who pays, say, $1,000 to take part in this game will almost inevitably find himself in profit after a relatively small number of plays. (If you don't believe this, try it at home using the sides of a coin to represent the two outcomes.)

Now if we look at the same calculation for the Hotel Infinity game:

Number of tosses until a tail (N)	Probability of N	Prize Expected	Payoff (prize divided by probability)
1	1/2	$2	$1
2	1/4	$4	$1
3	1/8	$8	$1
4	1/16	$16	$1
5	1/32	$32	$1
6	1/64	$64	$1
7	1/128	$128	$1
8	1/256	$256	$1
9	1/512	$512	$1
10	1/1024	$1,024	$1
n -> infinity	$1/2^n$	$\$2^n$	$1 ->infinity
Value of Game			$Infinite

This shows that given that the expected value of the game is the sum of the expected payoffs of all the possible outcomes (as we saw in our simplified version), and given that there are an infinite number of possible outcomes (since it is possible for the game to continue indefinitely), the expected payoff is an infinite number of dollars!

This means that a rational gambler should be willing to pay any finite amount of money to enter the game. Except, of course, that no rational gambler would be so willing, which is why this conclusion is seen as paradoxical.

Inspector Horse explains to George McClellan that the paradox is called the St. Petersburg Paradox, and that it has been troubling mathematicians and philosophers for nearly three hundred years. He indicates that the explanation for the paradox probably lies in the psychology of risk-aversion— the fact that we're not willing to gamble significant money on the miniscule chance of winning an unfathomably large fortune. However, he suggests that the fact that Hotel Infinity has an infinite number of guests probably means that they are right that the game will make some of their patrons very rich indeed.

PARADOX OF THE COURT SOLUTION

This is a version of a dilemma known as the Paradox of the Court, which is normally associated with the Greek sophist Protagoras. However, it is generally considered not to be a genuine paradox, and compared to some of the paradoxes of Ancient Greece its resolution is not too taxing.

A court should not find in favor of Lock Haven Law School. Winepol has a contract with the school which states that his fees are payable only when he wins his first case. He has not yet won a case, so the fees are not payable. However, Professor Protagoras is right to think that the consequence of Winepol's victory in this case would be that his fees become payable. Therefore, if the school were to launch a second case against Winepol—in the event that Winepol refused to pay the fees having won the first case—it would surely win it.

However, though Protagoras has come up with a clever ruse to force Winepol to pay his fees, in the real world it might not work out in the school's favor to proceed in this manner. Not least, it seems entirely possible that a judge would award costs to Winepol after his court victory, in which case the law school would almost certainly owe Winepol more than he owed it, since part of Winepol's costs is precisely the amount of the fees he has now had to pay to the school.

BURIDAN'S ASS SOLUTION

Inspector Horse is wrong to claim that the scenario he has outlined, known as the paradox of Buridan's Ass, demonstrates that human beings have free will and that causal determinism is false. However, there is no doubt that it poses a significant challenge for the view that all our behavior is determined by prior causes.

The problem is that it does seem to be the case that if causal determinism is true then a person standing precisely in the middle of two identical food sources, where there is nothing to incline him towards one rather than the other, will be unable to decide which food source to approach. However, it also seems to be true that if somebody was actually in this situation they would be able to make a choice. Therefore, it seems we are required to argue that causal determinism is false in order to escape the paradox.

However, although this argument is persuasive it is not conclusive. Consider, for example, that one might simply claim that if a person really did find themselves in this situation then they would not be able to choose. In other words, it is possible to bite the bullet here, and accept what seems to be highly counterintuitive: namely, that a person might starve to death rather than make a choice. Of course, there is no inconsistency in also arguing that this situation could never arise in real life. It seems entirely plausible that there will always be some factor in our causal history, or in the situation, which would provide the basis for a decision. Perhaps, for example, the fact that we are right-handed rather than left-handed, or the particular way that the light is falling across the food sources.

Therefore, although Inspector Horse has made a strong case for rejecting causal determinism, he has not conclusively proved that it is false. Moreover, there is some scientific evidence that indicates that free will might be an illusion, and that something like causal determinism might be true. In particular, work by Benjamin Libet suggests that voluntary acts are initiated unconsciously in the brain before we are even aware that we want to act. It is possible then that Hector House is right, and that he is not culpable for the attempted theft of the pedigree tortoise.

NEWCOMB'S PARADOX SOLUTION

The game that Frosty Reading is being asked to play is based on a thought experiment devised by the physicist William Newcomb in 1960. There is no generally accepted solution, and it remains the subject of considerable debate to this day. It is, nevertheless, possible to identify two main lines of argument that support opposing strategies.

The first line of argument states that it would be absurd for Reading to do anything other than take only Box B. He knows that the clairvoyant is accurate in her predictions. It follows that he is as good as guaranteed to gain $1,000,000 if he takes only Box B. However, if he takes Box A as well, it will turn out that Box B is empty, so he will lose the million dollars it would have contained had he not taken both boxes.

This seems an entirely plausible argument.

The trouble is that there is a second line of argument that supports the opposite conclusion and also seems entirely plausible. This argument holds that Reading should obviously take both boxes. By the time he makes his choice, the clairvoyant has already made her prediction, and the amount of money in the boxes is fixed. This means that it makes absolutely no difference to the outcome whether he takes one or two boxes. It follows, then, that Reading will always get an extra $10,000 by taking both boxes, which is the case whether Box B is empty or contains a million dollars. After all, if Box B is empty, it will remain empty, even if he takes only it away with him.

Of course, the arguments and counterarguments don't stop here—there is much more to be said for and against both views. However, there is no definitive solution to the dilemma. Probably there is a slight preference amongst philosophers for the second line of argument, which is based on what is known as the dominance principle. However, the first argument, which normally makes use of something called an expected utility hypothesis (a complex way of estimating people's betting preferences), also has its vociferous supporters.

THE SURPRISE PARTY SOLUTION

Clare has hit upon a form of argument, known as backward induction, that often features in the context of a story about an unexpected examination or hanging. The first point to make here is that she should not be so confident that her party is not going to take place. If she is convinced that it cannot occur, her parents can arrange for the party to happen at any point during the week, and she will be surprised.

Arguably, the more interesting question here is whether or not Clare's reasoning is correct. On the one hand, it seems obvious that a surprise party is *de facto* a possibility: we don't really think that somebody could not be surprised by a party given within a five-day timeframe. On the other hand, it is very difficult to say where Clare's reasoning has gone awry (indeed, some people claim that this is one of the more intractable philosophical conundrums).

A possible response is to argue that although the backward induction argument gets started, it doesn't go very far. Michael Clark, for example, suggests that on Wednesday evening, there is an instability in the argument which makes it possible to be surprised by the party on Thursday. The idea is that on Wednesday the thought will occur that perhaps the promise of a *surprise* party will be unfulfilled, which leaves open the possibility that the party will occur on either Thursday or Friday. In this situation, it is not possible to be certain that the party will happen on Thursday (since it might happen on Friday, although it won't be a surprise), which means that if it does happen on the Thursday, it will be a surprise. Once this is conceded, then all the earlier days are also possible dates for a surprise party.

THE LOTTERY PARADOX SOLUTION

This paradox suggests an easy solution: it is not the case that we believe a particular ticket will not win the lottery. Rather what we believe is that it is overwhelmingly likely that it will not win. Not only does this eradicate the paradox, it seems also to be borne out by the thought that part of what we come to know when we watch a lottery draw is that particular tickets have not won. If this is correct, then Alex Gibbon is being disingenuous when he claims that he does not believe his ticket will win. In reality, he just thinks it very unlikely.

However, there is a problem with this response. Consider the following scenario. You switch on your television and find that there is no picture. You switch channels, but still no picture. You continue to switch channels until you have been through all the major network stations, but you can't get a picture. You conclude that there is something wrong with the television or the cable service. You do *not* believe, and it seems rational not to believe, that all the networks have simultaneously stopped broadcasting. Yet this is a theoretical possibility. Indeed, it is probably more likely than the 14 million to one chance that a particular ticket will win the lottery.

The point here, of course, is that the belief that the networks have not stopped broadcasting seems rational. It does not appear that the only rational belief is that it is incredibly unlikely that the networks have stopped broadcasting. By assuming that the set is broken, you disregard the small possibility that the networks have stopped broadcasting. However, if this is right then it seems it must also to apply to the belief that no individual ticket will win the lottery, which brings the paradox crashing back in again.

THE SLEEPING BEAUTY PROBLEM SOLUTION

The Sleeping Beauty problem, as this thought-experiment is called, is a relatively complex puzzle in probability theory.

Perhaps the most intuitive answer is that there is a 50-50 chance that the coin came up heads. The thought here is that the only knowledge available to Sleeping Beauty on waking is the fact that a fair coin has been tossed, and that it came up either heads or tails. Nothing about the situation she now finds herself in tells her anything new about this probability, in which case she should conclude that the chance of the coin having fallen on heads is one-half.

However, there is a large complication here in the guise of the response that claims that Sleeping Beauty should conclude that the probability that a head came up is one-third. Imagine that the experiment has been conducted 1,000 times. Given a perfectly fair coin, this would give you 500 heads and 500 tails. However, the crucial point is that from the perspective of Sleeping Beauty she wakes up twice as often after the coin has landed tails than she does after it has landed heads.

COIN LANDS	NUMBER OF OCCASIONS	WOKEN ON MONDAY	WOKEN ON TUESDAY	TOTAL NUMBER OF TIMES WOKEN
HEADS	500	500		500
TAILS	500	500	500	1,000

This shows that if the experiment is conducted 1,000 times, Sleeping Beauty will wake after a head has been thrown on 500 occasions, compared to 1,000 occasions after a tail has been thrown. This suggests that she should estimate that the probability that the coin came up heads is one-third.

There is no universally accepted right answer to this problem, though the balance of opinion seems to be coming down on the side of the 'thirders'. If you want to give this conundrum some further thought, consider the following scenario. Rather than being woken on two consecutive days, Sleeping Beauty is woken on 499 consecutive days if the coin lands on tails. Now, on her awakening, what probability should she assign to the coin having landed on heads?

1. Fill the five gallon container, then use it to fill the three gallon container, which will leave two gallons in the five gallon container. Empty the three gallon container, and then pour the two gallons left in the five gallon container into it. Then refill the five gallon container, before using it to fill the three gallon container (which already has two gallons of water in it). This will leave four gallons in the five gallon container.

2. Eighty minutes is an hour and twenty minutes.

3. His younger son leapt on his brother's horse.

4. It's impossible for Rachel to average 60 miles per hour overall. She can only double her average speed for the whole journey if she does the return leg in no time at all. (She's already taken enough time so that any additional time will take her average speed below 60 miles per hour.)

CHAPTER 2

5. You need to use a little algebra to work this one out. Fifty-eight eyes means that there are twenty-nine animals in total. Let x equal the number of elephants, and 29 - x (number of animals minus the number of elephants) equal the number of emus. Then:

$4x + 2(29-x) = 84$	4x because each elephant has 4 legs; 2(29-x) because each emu has two legs; 84 legs in total.
$4x + 58 - 2x = 84$	Get rid of the brackets (multiply 29 and -x by 2).
$2x = 26$	Subtract 2x from 4x (on the left) and then 58 from both sides.
$x = 13$	Divide both sides by 2, giving the number of elephants.

There are thirteen elephants and, therefore, sixteen emus ($13 + 16 = 29$ animals).

6. The bowl was half full one minute earlier.

7. There are three swans.

8. The two boys are two of a set of triplets.

9. You should ask either one of the guards what the other guard would tell you if you asked him which door led to the pot of gold. Whatever he answers, the pot of gold will be behind the other door. (If you ask the guard who always tells the truth, he will truthfully tell you what the liar would have told you, so you know it's not that door. If you ask the guard who always lies, he will lie about what the truthful guard would have told you, so you know it isn't that door.)

10. There are 40,320 ways to arrange the books. You have eight books to choose from for the first book, seven for the second book, six for the third book, and so on, all the way down to the last book:

$$8 \times 7 \times 6 \times 5 \times 4 \times 3 \times 2 \times 1 = 40,320.$$

CHAPTER 4

11. Thirty-two players take part in the tournament.

Round	Total Matches	Total Players
Final	1	2
Semi-final	(1+2) = 3	4
Quarter-final	(1+2+4) = 7	8
2nd round	(1+2+4+8) = 15	16
1st round	(1+2+4+8+16) = 31	32

12. The man is very short, and cannot reach higher than the elevator button for the eighth floor, except if it is raining, when he is able to use his umbrella to hit the tenth floor button.

CHAPTER 5

13. It is seven A.M. in the morning. You know the clock was right at two A.M., and that it stopped when it showed the time as eight twenty-four A.M. In its terms, it worked for a total of six hours and twenty-four minutes—or 384 minutes—before stopping. Every ninety-six of those minutes is one hour in real terms (the clock gains thirty-six minutes every hour). A bit of long division tells you that this is four hours (386 ÷ 96). This means that the clock stopped (one hour ago) at six A.M. So the time is now seven A.M.

14. Three of the soldiers must have all the injuries. The total number of injuries is 153. If all fifty soldiers have three injuries, it leaves three injuries unaccounted for. Therefore, three soldiers out of the fifty must have all four injuries.

CHAPTER 6

15. Both children must be lying since if only one of them were lying then they would both be the same sex, yet we know that a boy and a girl are sitting together on the bench. Since both are lying it means that the child with blonde hair is the boy, and the child with brown hair is the girl.

16. The farmer takes the chicken across first, and then comes back for the fox. He takes the fox across, but crucially brings the chicken back with him on the return journey. He then takes the grain across, leaving the chicken behind, returning one final time to collect the chicken. At no time is the chicken left alone with the grain, or the fox with the chicken (which is a huge relief to both the chicken and the grain).

17. Seven people are at the reunion: two girls and a boy, their parents, and their father's parents.

18. No, the dead can't get married.

19. You put the following weights onto the scales: one weight from the first set, two from the second set, three from the third set, and so on. Then if the expected total weight is one kilogram out, you know that the fault lies in the first set, if it is two kilograms out then the fault lies in the second set, and so on.

INDEX